PAINT EFFECTS

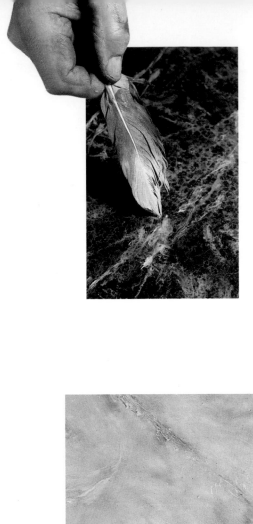

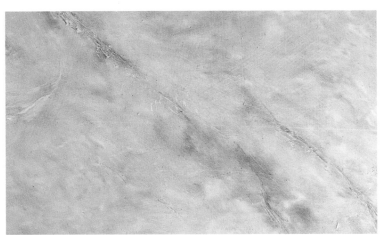
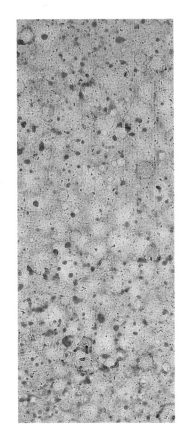
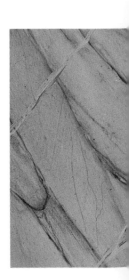

PAINT
EFFECTS

EMMA CALLERY

CHARTWELL
BOOKS, INC.

A QUINTET BOOK

Published by
Chartwell Books
A Division of Book Sales, Inc.
110 Enterprise Avenue
Secaucus, New Jersey 07094

ISBN 1-55521-949-7

This book was designed and produced by
Quintet Publishing Limited
6 Blundell Street
London N7 9BH

Creative Director: Peter Bridgewater
Art Director: Ian Hunt
Project Editor: Emma Callery
Editor: Lindsay Porter

Typeset in Great Britain by
Central Southern Typesetters, Eastbourne
Manufactured in Hong Kong by
Regent Publishing Services Limited
Printed in Hong Kong by
Leefung Asco Printers Limited

The material in this publication previously
appeared in *Paint Finishes* and
Surfaces and Finishes

CONTENTS

INTRODUCTION

Paint has greater versatility than any other surface finish. It not only offers infinite variety of colour and texture, it also affords protection to the surface – and does both at less cost than any other decorative material. Its chromatic and textural variety also allows it to evoke other materials, be they wood, marble or other polished stones, tortoiseshell or fabric; paint can be transparent or opaque; it can even offer images of objects that are not there.

This book is about paint and the effects it offers which may be achieved by the amateur with imagination, care and enthusiasm. Most of the decorative techniques described are applicable to furniture as well as to walls, ceilings and floors. For instance, marbling may seem the preserve of walls, but can add panache to tables or kitchen units. Spattering – or its more specialized variant, porphyry – is as effective on bathroom fittings as on coffee tables. Picking-out can reveal the shape of mouldings, cornices, or turned and scrolled chair legs, that have been rendered formless by bad painting.

Because of its great variety and versatility – and ease of application – paint needs to be used with discretion. Over-spicing the cake is as easy when creating a colour recipe as when mixing a culinary one. Using too many different effects in a room – on the walls or furniture – can detract from the overall look and become confusing. It's easy to avoid this error. In observing a room and the objects in it, take into account three things: look first at the shape of the room and its proportions, which will influence what you should paint and how; the fall of light, which will affect

the colours you choose; and the structural condition of the room and its contents, which will dictate the preparation of the surfaces to be painted. For example, in a room with variously shaped woodwork panelling, it's a mistake to marble the walls and give a mottled, broken colour pattern like rag-rolling to the wood; the clash of effects would destroy form and create visual chaos. Colours are important, too; those which make a north-facing room warm may make a south-facing room quite overpowering. Finally, the finish must be suited to its context: applying marbling to furniture that has the lightness of bamboo looks like the old music hall joke about the featherweight dumb-bell – totally unsuitable and so unpleasing to the eye.

To turn paint's versatility to your best advantage, it's useful to know something about the structure of colour, so that you can mix paint; materials, and the tasks they are suited to; and how to prepare the surfaces you wish to paint. The first three chapters will lead you through these planning stages. The following three describe all the various effects and finishes you can get, where to use them and how to achieve them. With a little care, you can create a whole new look, from spattering a foot-stool to wood graining the floor of the hall.

All rooms, like all people, look different. Even in a tower block with identically structured rooms, no two are the same; this is because each room is at a different height or has a different orientation, so the light in each is different. Light affects the way that colours strike the eye, so suiting your

LEFT *Ensure colour works with furniture and decorative objects to create a harmonious total effect; one dominating feature could disrupt the balance of the room.*

LEFT *When choosing paint, the first priority is colour. Paint comes in every hue of the spectrum, giving a range of patterns and tones beyond imagination. To make the best use of this variety and to derive the greatest pleasure from paint in interior decoration, it is necessary to know the basics of how colour works.*

BELOW *Large areas of primary colours used together dictate to everything around them but can be very striking.*

choice of colours to the prevailing light is vital. It is colour that gives a room its identity. There is almost no such thing as an ugly room; virtually any room, well painted, can look good. A beautifully painted room will look beautiful even if there's nothing else in it. (Indeed, over-furnishing detracts from a room, by confusing the colour and the fall of light, and in extreme cases wrecking the proportions and form of the space.) It is colour that gives a room brightness, warmth or coolness, drama, elegance or playfulness; it is colour as much as shape that gives a room 'atmosphere', for it is the fall of light and the luxury of our colour vision that give the world visible form and ambiance. The sheer range and panache of colour can intimidate people – when they do not take it for granted – and yet the basic principles of colour are very simple.

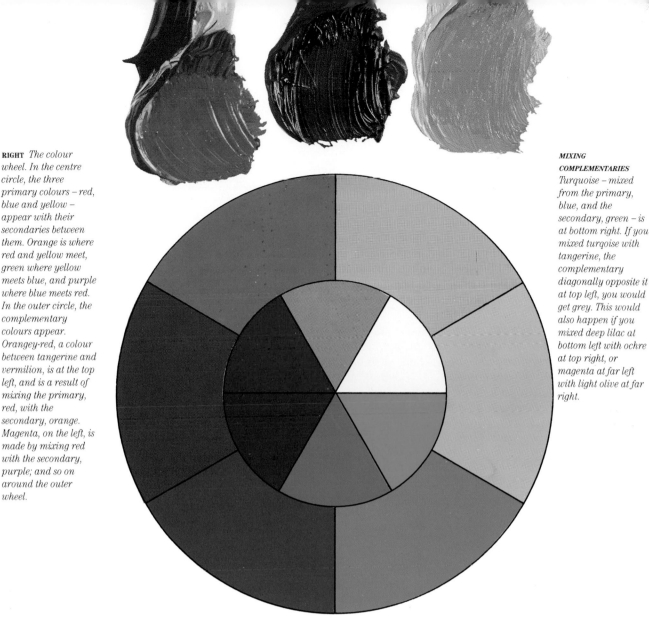

COLOUR THEORY

Most of us learn in school about the structure of colour, set out on a colour wheel, and then swiftly forget about it; so a brief resumé will be useful. There are two main sets of colour rules: those of light mixing, which must be applied when laying one colour over another as in glazing; and those of pigment mixing, which control results when physically mixing different coloured paints. Some terminology may be useful: the primary colours – red, blue and yellow – are often referred to as hues. When a pigment is lightened with white, it is strictly called a tint, and when darkened with black, a shade, so pink is a tint of red, and mustard is a shade of yellow. In practice, though, on manufacturers' colour charts and in magazines and in other publications, the terms 'tones' and 'tonal values' have become widespread to describe the level of lightness or darkness of a colour. These terms are useful because manufacturers produce scores of variations of, say, blue, to which they give registered tradenames; all of them are really a basic blue – say, ultramarine – with different amounts of white or black added, and sometimes both white and black added at the same time, giving a greyer blue. These are all tones. This term is useful, too, when you wish to describe a mixture of different colours in a room which all have the same intensity, for example; pink and sky-blue. They are different colours but neither is more intense than the other; they both have an equal amount of white pigment in them, so they are called tonally equal; and therefore neither colour will dominate the room.

The primary colours – red, blue and yellow – are so called because you can't make them by mixing other colours. On the other hand, basic colour theory tells us that from these primaries all the other colours can be made. This isn't strictly true, but all other colours contain two of the primaries and the primaries do produce the vast majority of colours. Red and yellow make orange; blue and yellow make green; blue and red, purple. These are secondary colours. If you mix two secondary colours you get a tertiary colour. Olive is a tertiary, a mixture of purple and green. Tints and shades are produced by adding black and/or white to a primary, secondary or tertiary colour. With the addition of black or white, of course, colours lack the brilliance or intensity of primaries and secondaries. Beige, for instance, is a tertiary paled with white.

Colours are usually arranged on a chromatic scale and displayed on colour charts, but the famous 'wheel' remains the most effective way of demonstrating the structure of colour. These colours which appear opposite each other on the wheel, or nearly so, are called 'complementary'. This is because when they are mixed in equal quantities they cancel each other out and, rather surprisingly, you get grey as a result. Mix red and turquoise in slightly different proportions and you will get variations of grey. The same thing will happen with blue and orange. (This is assuming that the pigments are pure – in fact, most commercial complementary paints are not pure and will produce a muddy khaki when mixed.)

When you place true complementaries side by side you get a 'buzz' – the colours seem to overlap each other in a narrow, grey blur. This phenomenon can be useful in decorating; a harsh colour of any type can be softened by adding to it a small amount of its complementary. A particularly stark red on a north-facing wall can be softened to a warmer, weathered brick-red by adding a little turquoise, and orange does the same for a hard, chilly blue.

Of course, artificially produced colours available today have a brilliance which cannot be achieved by hand-mixing primaries and secondaries

yourself. But if you seek to understand colour, there is no substitute for mixing it yourself. You cannot, for instance, 'think' a colour. You can imagine scenes in colour, of course – just as you may dream in colour – but can you reproduce the colour you imagine? Assuredly not. Colours are seen in relation to light and other contingent colours, so a colour visualized in the abstract lacks a defining context. That is why when you see a colour in your mind's eye and go looking for it on a colour chart, you so often can't find it; the colour is only in the mind and is isolated from other colours around you. It has no physical existence.

Another excellent way of learning about colour, especially if you are trying to decide on a colour scheme for a room, is just to experiment with a water-colour paint box, painting blocks of colour, and holding them up, sight-size (until they block out the area you want to paint) to the appropriate part of the room. This can save you time – and a fortune in paint. You can also discover interesting colour combinations that you may have been conditioned into thinking don't go together, like making delicate olives from purples and greens, or juxtaposing blue and green.

Of course, you don't have to mix the pigments of colours together to change them. It is generally admitted that colour is at its most beautiful in its transparent state, applied over a white ground, with light shining through the colour. Hold up a 35mm colour slide to a light source and it is luminous, like stained glass, because the light shines through it. Almost all colours that artists use are transparent. Only a few are opaque – namely vermilion, cerulean blue, emerald green, ochre and some yellows. If you apply artists' paint directly from a tube and mix it with either water or mineral spirits, the original purity is never lost. Glaze painting is a technique involving overlaying one of these transparent colours with another or applying a

transparent colour over a white ground. It is a very ancient way of painting and retains the purity of the colours. Glaze painting is similar to the modern four-colour printing process, where the various gradations of colour are obtained by printing one colour over another, on a ground of white paper.

Painting a picture in glazes is a more complicated process than painting by mixing pigments, but there are few such problems in using the technique for the paint finishes described in this book. All you need to know is that if you mix a transparent colour and apply it over another colour, that process is called glazing and there are certain formal colour rules that it is useful to know.

In the glaze technique the aim is just the opposite from that in pigment mixing: transparency is essential for maximum effectiveness, so only transparent colours are used. Starting with a white ground, the painter covers the area with thin layers of transparent paint, which act as colour filters. The white light shining down through them is reflected back up and out again from the white ground below. The more glazes that are put on, the less light is reflected back up, so the area appears progressively darker. You can go on until you get black but you will never get mud colour; glazes retain a 'clean' appearance down to the lowest levels of illumination.

In glazing, you are effectively removing various areas of white light; so you can no longer use the rules of pigment mixing described earlier, but must go by the rules of light mixing. To begin with, sunlight is white (strictly speaking a non-colour) unless it is separated with a prism into the colours of the rainbow. When it is separated, it divides into pure colours, that is, colours that are undiluted and are therefore at their maximum intensity. These include the three primaries – red, blue and yellow. The primary colours for light mixing are orange (sometimes defined as red-yellow), green and blue. The complementary colour of orange is blue-green, of blue is yellow, and of green is violet.

The basic rules of light mixing are: to soften a colour, use a thin glaze of its complementary light colour; to intensify it, add a second glaze of the same colour. Blue over yellow still makes green, red over yellow, orange; *but* red over blue-green makes olive. So, for example, if you have an apple green wall you can give it a transparent glaze of rose colour and create the same kind of mellow light that you see on a green tree on a sunny, late summer afternoon. If you mixed the same rose-coloured paint in the can with green pigment, you'd get the kind of colour you see on an army lorry. Similarly, glazing pure rose madder (deep rose) over a white ground gives a clear, deep rose. Mix rose madder paint with white pigment, though, and you'll end up with a paler pink. The result with mixed pigments is a surface colour, not a transparent one; a colour you can look *on* to but not *into*.

USING ▓▓▓▓▓

▓▓▓▓▓ *COLOR*

Because all rooms vary, there is no universally applicable recipe for a successful interior; but there are more and less effective ways of using colour. There is a simple way to observe a room and see what its problems are: walk about and look at all its different angles, paying special attention to the view from the door as you enter. Note the proportions: the height and width. Is the room too high or too low for its size? Are the doors symmetrically placed? Should they be made a feature, or should they be made to blend so as not to detract from the proportions of the room? Are the windows large, small, positioned oddly, too high or too low? Which way do they face? Look at the light from the windows: what will it be like at other times of the day? Will it be cold, clear, north light or warm southern or western? All these considerations should affect your choice of colour and finish. If areas are broken with alcoves, hatches and recesses, or interspersed with windows of varying heights and widths, the room will benefit from unity of colour and finish. The woodwork at least should be integrated with the walls, and not finished in a markedly contrasting colour or style, otherwise the variousness becomes disturbing, dictating to you rather than providing a pleasant environment.

When the quality of light is cold, such as in a dark, north-facing room, a common approach is to attempt to lighten and warm it with brilliant colour. This frequently overwhelms the interior. What north light lacks is mellowness, so the harsh, deep reds – poppy and geranium – do not work well; they look bloody rather than warm in the grey light. Softer colour, like brick-red, lightens and warms the room without being overpowering. A cold, green room can be glazed with red, or a red one with green, to produce amber-olives. Blues, greens and greys can all be darkened for depth and given a warm under-toning by choosing a shade with a touch of red or yellow; their tendency to coldness can be offset with mustards, mellow terracottas and warm earth colours.

Sunny, southern-facing rooms can become too yellow; an excess of 'sunny' colours can make them poky, like teapots full of tannin. They often benefit from cooler colouring; an almost-white pale pink or a very pale green can work very well.

This brings us to the one thing which all artists tend to presume is common knowledge – that some colours are considered cold and others warm. Blues and greens are usually the cool ones; reds and yellows warm. The reason for this is very simple. Colour, as any astronomer will tell you, is divided into short and long wavelengths. Blue is a short-wavelength colour, so it seems to recede; it looks far away, so a blue room looks cool because it reminds us of distance and space. There are visual associations too; the blue sky, the sea and distant mountain-tops are all blue, and cool. The more yellow blue has in it, the warmer and more summery it looks. Red is a long-wavelength colour, so it

LEFT *The informal harmony of this room relies on the use of a single overall colour. The walls are accented by very small, precise stencils.*

RIGHT *Painted wood graining gives a crisp framing to this cool, varnished, off-white interior; the stark, clean lines of the furniture demand a visual balance on the walls and doors; plain painted surfaces would run the risk of becoming extremely heavy. Wood graining gives weight and variety without looking oppressive.*

seems to come towards us and looks close; it's therefore associated with warmth. Visual associations strengthen the sensation of heat – fire, the colour of the red-brown earth, blood and life.

A lot of these associations are subconscious and very ancient, and it is easy to forget that because light is the cause of colour, light changes colour. To assume – as many people do – that because a colour is associated with warmth it is automatically going to make a place look warm is logical but, unfortunately, not necessarily correct.

Warmth can become heavy and coolness bleak. These effects are highly subjective.

There is no worse way of approaching a colour scheme than as a rigorous intellectual exercise. The trouble is, we're conditioned by our society to take a logical, analytical approach to problems and to distrust our instincts and feelings as whimsical, self-indulgent, even as a sign of weakness. Choosing colour, however, is all about instinctive feeling in relation to light. 'Overthink' is one of the reasons so many

COLOUR EFFECTS WITH GLAZES

Most colours are transparent. The yellows, vermilion, emerald and cerulean blue are not. Glazing is painting in transparent colour. If you thin paint with solvent – mineral spirits or water – this is called a paint glaze; if with glaze – a transparent gel available from paint suppliers – it is called tinted glaze. Paint glazes make semi-opaque washes; tinted glazes, translucent top coats.

people have problems with colour. They hear that dark blue is synonymous with dignity, strength and quiet dynamism, and so, psychologically, it is: it is a holy colour to the Buddhists, not to mention the colour of about half the world's dress uniforms, but that doesn't mean it's going to work well on a south-facing living room wall. Cover walls with it in that light, and you'll end up feeling like a parking ticket in a policeman's blue pocket. Similarly, if you paint a north-facing room scarlet, the cold light will make the colour stark and it won't feel any more vital and warm than being walled up inside a fire engine; paint it bright lemon and you'll know what fruit juice in the freezer goes through.

There are two sorts of colour relationship that it's wise to avoid, not because they are wrong but because they often cause other problems. This is what they are and how to remedy them.

OFF-HUES

When placed side by side, true contrasting colours do not alter your perception of their colour; that is to say, vermilion red looks just as red, cerulean blue just as blue, and they also strengthen and intensify each other. On the other hand, colours more similar to one another but not actually adjacent on the colour wheel – such as

ultramarine blue and one of the red-purples, such as rose madder – send each other off-hue when they are placed side by side. These make very uncomfortable colour combinations in a room. They can, however, be transformed by playing around with the proportions of pigment by which they're made and by using other tones that lie between them; they can be linked by unusual and fascinating series of decorating colours. The difficulty with this is that if you have used large areas of contrasting colours, you will either have to use many smaller painted surfaces with the intermediary tones, or else use other materials to supply the link. Try to avoid large areas of true contrasting colours. They can be very

disturbing in directly adjacent positions. Alternatively, they can be very effective if you have a large area of one, and the other in very small areas against it.

DISCORDANT COLOURS

These are produced when the sequence of light and dark colours as they appear on the colour wheel are unbalanced by adding an equal amount of white to the darker colours and black to the light ones, so that their relationships are reversed. A typical grotesque discord would be achieved by adding black to yellow – making mustard – and then adding white to a deep blue; used in equal quantities, this combination may turn your stomach and set you craving

for tinted glasses. Again, the prime remedy for this is that very small areas of one colour can work against large areas of the other – like a scattered pattern on fabric. Never use discordant colours in equal measure against one another.

Colour is not a tyrant that cannot be placated until the personality of the individual decorating the room has been removed – quite the contrary. The mere fact that colour gives so vast a choice ensures that the choice reflects individual personality. So too, does subtlety of colour. Subtle colours are assertive precisely because they leave room for additions of stylistic panache and leave the options open for everything from quiet elegance to high drama.

Once you've settled on a colour scheme, choose a finish that is suited to it, and to the surfaces you intend to paint. Wood graining a chair in navy blue and turquoise looks eccentric, to say the least; sponging a wall in olive and yellow will make you feel like you're under fire. As each technique is described, the pros and cons of its various uses are discussed. It's worth giving careful thought to the choice of finish and colours before you start, to ensure a pleasing, congruent unity in the finished effect.

PAINTING

Although there is a greater variety of paint available now, there are only two basic types: water-based and oil-based. All paint consists of coloured particles – pigment – held together in a binding solution, which is soluble in either oil or water. The great majority of water-based paints are not shiny when dry, about half of the oil-based paints are.

For the purposes of interior decoration, most people are interested in what type of finish the paint will give, so manufacturers categorize paints according to the degree of shine they have.

LEFT *Ragging gives a damask-like or white velvet texture to these walls where a plain surface would be excessively neutral. But the walls must be 'quiet' as the warm honey-ochre tones of other surfaces are gentle and discreet in themselves, while having a very distinct tactile quality.*

SINGLE COLOUR ROOMS

In interiors with many colourful objects, such as books, it's often a mistake to use more than two colours for walls and woodwork, and a single colour for both can lend a pleasing visual unity. Nonetheless, the basic hue of a single-colour room must be chosen with care. Dark walls – say, deep blue – need pale, relieving woodwork, but pale walls don't normally need dark woodwork. Mid-tone walls can have either dark or light wooden areas, but usually require some defining contrast. Rooms where wood and walls are all one colour look odd with a contrasting ceiling.

Those with no shine are called flat or matt paints; those with a slight shine are low-lustre, eggshell, silk-finish or satin-finish; and those with a high shine, gloss or high-gloss.

Having discussed the variety of paints available and the different effects they will achieve, it is necessary to consider where to apply which paint. This is largely a matter of taste, but there are a few points to bear in mind. It isn't a good idea to put high-gloss or the more shiny low-lustre paints on a wall with lumps or undulations because the paint will highlight the flaws. High-gloss paint on woodwork adjoining a matt wall draws too much attention to the woodwork and makes the walls appear to recede. Gloss paint washes more easily than other types, but woodwork tends to look better with low-lustre or matt. If you need to protect paint from constant handling – on a banister or door, for example – it is preferable to varnish it. Three coats of varnish over matt paint are no more likely to chip than a thick coat of gloss paint; also, gloss has a hard, cold, colourless shine, whereas flat paint that has been varnished retains a gleam of its own colour where it catches the light.

MATT OR FLAT PAINTS

■ *Flat-oil* Widely used by professional decorators, this is the best paint for all interior surfaces; its consistency, coverage and finish are superior to all other paints. In the UK, flat-oil is available only through specialist suppliers. An undercoat is essential for a good finish with this and all other oil-based paints. Two thin top coats are better than one thick one; they are easier to brush on evenly and they adhere better. Using mineral spirits, thin the paint until it holds to the brush like thin cream, but never more. Don't thin top coats as much. It is best to apply the paint fairly liberally, brush it to a thin, even film and then lay off carefully.

■ *Undercoat* Undercoat is an oil-based paint, used to provide a non-porous ground for all oil-based finishing coats. It is not usually applied as a top coat itself, but it can be substituted for flat-oil if necessary. If you do this, you may need two coats (as undercoat covers the surface more thinly than flat-oil) and you should protect it with a coat or two of matt varnish because its powdery texture makes it less durable than top coat paint. The colour range is limited, but the colours are quite subtle and the paint is easily tinted.

Undercoat is an excellent base for over-decorating techniques, such as marbling, but you should buy one of the better quality brands for this, as they dry to a smoother finish. The first application of undercoat may be thinned half-and-half with mineral spirits to saturate a porous surface and to create a key for the next, full-strength coat.

■ *Latex* This term is used to describe a wide range of water-based paints which are usually applied to plaster; the range now includes matt vinyls also known as latex flat enamels. You cannot apply latexes to metal as, being porous, they will allow it to corrode. They aren't really suitable as a ground for over-decoration, either (unless sealed with a matt varnish), but they are good for washes because they can easily be thinned with water. Latexes are relatively inexpensive and are easy to use. They dry quickly and can easily be covered with other types of paint to avoid porosity. Lately latexes have been produced to withstand steamy atmospheres, too.

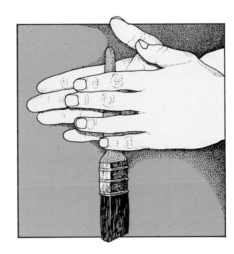

You can apply latexes over new plaster, as they will let it breathe; they also have good adhesion and very little smell. A 'mist' coat of latex on new plaster can be thinned 1:1 with water and the next coat applied at full strength. Apply this second coat liberally and don't over-brush. It's useful to lay off this paint toward a light source, rather than downward, to ensure an even appearance.

LOW-LUSTRE TO GLOSS

■ *Eggshell and low-lustre* These can be oil-based or water-based. The oil-based paints are non-porous and give a soft, expensive-looking sheen on walls or woodwork. They are suitable for over-painting and other decorative techniques. They look much better when applied in several well-thinned coats rather than one thick one, which will look heavy and rubbery. The water-based paints are really designed for walls; they are fast-drying, but don't wear as well as oil-based ones. On woodwork, water-based eggshells last longer than matt latexes. When thinned, their consistency should be no less than that of thin cream, and they should be applied with the same brushwork method as flat-oil. Both low-lustre and eggshell paints need an undercoat.

▌ *Trade eggshell* Like flat-oil, this oil-based paint is usually supplied only to the decorating trade and is superior to all other low-lustre paints. It is more expensive but more durable, hard and smooth with a better, even sheen and is suitable for doors, furniture and walls and as a ground for many over-decorating techniques. Although rather harder to work with than other low-lustre paints, demanding careful brushwork, the effect of trade eggshell is well worth the extra trouble. The methods of application are the same as for flat-oil.

▌ *Gloss* All gloss paints are oil-based. The terms semi-gloss, gloss, high-gloss, wet-look and hard-gloss describe different levels of shine. Normally, the shinier the paint is, the more durable it

will be. Gloss paints are highly resistant to water and dirt, although they do tend to chip. Gloss is usually applied to wood and metal and is often suitable for exterior use. It demands careful brushing on and laying off. These paints can be diluted with mineral spirits but they should not be thinned too much. The thinnest desirable texture is that of mayonnaise or tomato ketchup; any more thinning will break the consistency of the paint. Gloss paints need an undercoat and should then be laid on generously, over a small section of the surface at a time, and distributed evenly with cross-strokes. After this, tip off the brush on the edge of a paint kettle and then remove any excess paint. You can tell whether the application is even by the feel of the brush; it will slither greasily on saturated surfaces and drag over those that are too thinly covered. Use cross-strokes to correct any unevenness, and then lay off with firm, evenly pressured strokes. It's useful to apply successive coats in different directions to avoid a track effect. If you are painting on wood, always finish the last coat in the same direction as the grain.

USING GLOSS OVER LARGE AREAS

Woodwork and floors are the best surfaces for large areas of gloss, not walls. For shiny walls, use gloss varnish over flat-oil or latex. Finish is of paramount importance to gloss. When laying on, criss-cross the strokes to avoid tracks; then cross off feather-light finishing strokes with another brush, always going in the same direction. On wood, always follow the grain. On hardboard and similar surfaces, lay off toward the light. Don't use rollers; gloss tends to peel off when rolled, owing to insufficient adhesion.

Tinting means adding pigment to an already-mixed paint to alter the colour, or adding colour to varnish. The difference between ready-mixed decorating paint and pigments is that the first comes in bulk, ready for application, while pigments are colours sold in concentrated form. Pigments are soluble in either oil or water and can be thinned to different intensities. Never add pigment at a ratio of more than 1:8 to manufactured decorating paint, because the paint is already pigmented and may start to set. You should mix a sample after adding pigment and let it dry, because the colour will alter as it dries. Mix the main quantity when you get the colour you want on the dry sample.

OIL-BASED PIGMENTS

▌ *Artists' oils* Oils can be added to any oil-based paint and are available from art shops. They are rather expensive but they offer by far the most sophisticated of all colour ranges. The lowest prices are earth colours, such as brick-red and brown; the most expensive are the chrome yellows, cadmium reds and all the blues. Artists' oils are slow-drying and can be thinned with linseed oil, mineral spirits or turpentine. For tinting

LAYING OFF STROKES

Laying off should be done with a nearly dry brush, using long, even, very light strokes. It is often advisable to lay off toward a light source, but on woodwork – whether on walls, floors or furniture – the direction of the grain takes precedence. The brush should be held like a pen, when painting wood; a flat brush is suitable for parallel mouldings, an angled cutter-in for glazing bars or for fine details on furniture.

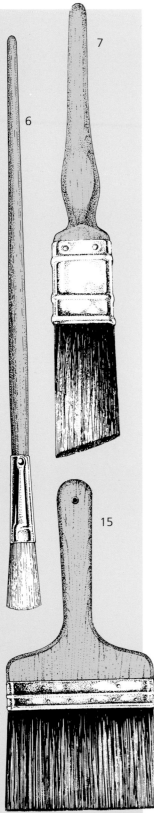

RIGHT *Laying off should be done with a nearly dry brush using long, even, very light strokes.*

wall-paints, a small amount should be mixed to a creamy consistency with mineral spirits, using a palette knife, and then stirred into the decorating paint. Oils can also be used to tint varnish: when tinting cheap varnish, oils should be diluted with a little linseed oil. Pigment spreads quickly in varnish, so only a little is needed. The pigment of cheaper oils is sometimes grittier than that of better quality ones. Good quality oils with a touch of linseed oil flow best.

WATER-BASED PIGMENTS

▌ *Artists' powder pigments* These are soluble in water. They are available in fewer colours than the oils but they are strong and clear. They dissolve less easily in water than poster colour (the other powder pigment), so there may be gritty particles that cause streaks; it's advisable to strain paint to which they've been added. They do, however, make excellent stains and washes.

▌ *Poster colours* These are rather heavy, crude, powder colours with a large amount of filler but they are correspondingly inexpensive and easy to mix. The amount of filler means that they're not very concentrated and so the colours are less harsh when mixed into the paint.

▌ *Artists' gouache* Professional artists, designers and illustrators use gouache. It is expensive but the colours are nearly as varied as those of artists' oils. Very concentrated and therefore opaque, gouaches make good stains and washes. In fact, they are probably the most versatile of all water-soluble pigments for washes.

▌ *Artists' acrylics* These are very good, water-soluble, plastic-based paints and were originally developed as a counterpart to artists' oils, intended for the large, 'sharp-edged' canvas paintings of the early 1960s. In practice, they offer a more limited colour range than oil or

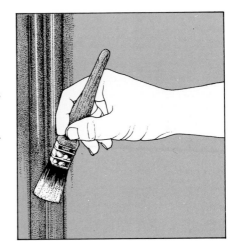

gouache. The range is limited in earth colours and neutrals, but is strong in mid-tones and pastels. Acrylics are not quite as expensive as oils, but you will need a greater quantity to paint the same area. They are very quick-drying; you can buy an effective retarder, but quick drying can be an asset in sharp-edged pattern-work like lining and stencilling.

▌ *Universal stainers* These are used by the decorating trade to tint water-based paints. They vary from one manufacturer to another but are all very concentrated, so a little goes a very long way. The colour range is limited and not very subtle but this is partly mitigated by the ease of mixing.

All water-soluble pigments should be protected by a coat of clear varnish if they've been used as a wash over colour already applied, so that they won't wash off. Some, such as the acrylics, are waterproof when dry and should not wash away, but it's always better to varnish a pigmented finish to be on the safe side, and prevent disappointments later.

VARNISHING

Many paint finishes will benefit both practically and aesthetically from varnishing. Varnish brings out the colours in the finishes rather as salt adds flavour to food, but it also protects the surface, essential in the case of any thinned water-based finish, which can otherwise easily rub off. Use matt, semi-gloss or gloss polyurethane varnish. Matt has the least sheen – although it is not completely flat – and is therefore the kindest to uneven walls. However, it is the least hard-wearing, so take the trouble to apply at least a couple of coats. Semi-gloss and gloss are harder-wearing, but their sheen will show up an imperfect surface as well as every speck of dust left on it before varnishing. You would be well advised to wash down the surface first, then vacuum the room thoroughly and keep doors and windows shut, both while you apply the varnish and until it is completely dry. You are less likely to get streaks or ridges with semi-gloss or gloss varnish if you thin it with one-third its quantity of mineral spirits. Diluting with mineral spirits has the additional advantage of making it easier to brush on. Always keep one brush for use with varnish only, so that there is no risk of old paint coming off on the new finish. It is worth taking the trouble in the first place, as you will only regret even the tiniest of faults in the varnish later.

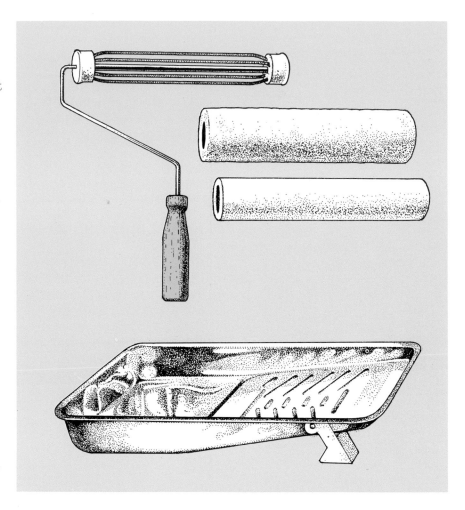

EQUIPMENT

BRUSHES

Plasterwork is best painted with flat wall-brushes of between 4in and 5in (10cm and 12.5cm), which should be held midway along the handle, like a knife. For woodwork, including furniture, brushes are usually held by the stock, between thumb and fingers, and it's best to have 3in, 2in and 1in (7.5cm, 5cm and 2.5cm) cutting-in brushes for window-frames, skirting boards, details and mouldings.

Always get the very best brushes you can afford, because the difference in performance between a good brush and a cheap one is enormous. It's also very important to look after them properly.

Clean a brush as soon as you buy it, even if it's wrapped in cellophane; it's a dirty world and even the best brushes have loose hairs. Twirl the brush with the handle between your palms, give it a good wash in mineral spirits and then twirl it dry. Break new brushes in by using them for priming and general preparation rather than for top coats, until all the short, loose hairs have come free. Brushes used with oil-based paint should be cleaned in mineral spirits, then washed in lukewarm, soapy water, rinsed and hung up to dry, bristles downward. Don't leave brushes with the bristles pointing upward because any remaining paint will drizzle deep into the hair roots, go hard, and cause a build-up of coagulated paint that separates the bristles until your brush looks like a moulting cockatoo. Brushes used with water-based paint should be rinsed off in cold water first, then washed in warm, soapy water, rinsed again and hung up to dry. Never leave brushes resting on their tips or the bristles will distort. Store them flat when dry. If you want to leave them overnight to continue painting in the morning, oil-paint brushes can be suspended in a 1:1 mixture of mineral spirits and raw linseed oil, with the container covered to keep out dust and air; before use, rinse them in solvent and twirl them dry. For a similar limited period, latex brushes can be kept damp in a polythene bag.

When painting with brushes, always proceed methodically and don't rush; and use two brushes, so that one is clean for finishing. Go section by section, laying on enough paint to cover a section, crossing the strokes to eliminate tracks and then laying off with a nearly dry brush in long, very light strokes in one direction (like using a feather duster) to get a smooth finish. Work sufficiently to ensure that the edges of the previous section are wet enough for you to brush the next one into it, but don't go back over a finished section or you'll ruin the texture.

Paint kettles enable you to use a small amount of paint at a time, while leaving the rest covered, which will protect it from gritty particles and prevent it from forming a skin. Don't immerse a brush up to the haft – it isn't necessary and clogs the bristles. Put the first inch or so of the bristles into the kettle and press each face of the brush against the side of the can to release excess paint. Don't wipe brushes on the rim, as this will form deposits that drop into the paint and make lumps. Use a nearly dry brush to take off any paint clinging to the inside walls.

ROLLERS

The advantage of rollers is their speed but this and the pile cause a superficial application of paint. This drawback is most pronounced with gloss paint, which can peel off in strips after roller application because of insufficient surface adhesion. For a textured surface, use a roller with a long pile; for general purposes, a medium pile; for very smooth surfaces, a short pile. As with brushes, buy the best you can afford. For high walls and ceilings, you'll need a roller with an extension handle.

The most common error in using rollers is overloading; an overloaded roller will spray paint everywhere like an exuberant wet puppy and squelch over the wall, leaving a texture like thin frogspawn. Avoid this by using a sloping paint tray and never filling more than one-third of its length with paint; any more, and the ribs on the bottom of the tray – which prevent overloading – won't work. After use, clean the roller in the

appropriate paint solvent, then wash it in lukewarm, soapy water, rinse it and hang it up to dry. Like brushes, rollers used with water-based paints can be kept moist in polythene for short periods.

SPRAY GUNS

Large commercial spray guns are a swift way to paint and have long been used for decorating new houses in America. Spraying with latex over new plaster is particularly rapid, as the mist or sealing coat and top coats may be applied in quick succession. The primer and undercoat of oil-based paint take longer but the finish of oil-based paints is usually enhanced by careful spraying and application of the top coat is quick. As when using brushes, two or three thinned coats give a better finish and adhesion than one thick, so the fact that you have to thin paint for spraying is an asset. Spray guns vary in size and weight from small, bottle-fed, torch-like objects, reminiscent of science fiction ray-guns – which are light, convenient and highly manoeuvrable but give a small area of coverage – to big, canister-fed ones with nozzles in a flexible tube. Their use, loading and the desirable consistency of paint varies – follow the manufacturer's instructions. The main drawback of spraying is the time consumed in masking windows and fittings, although this is outweighed by the subsequent speed of execution. Also, a fine mist of paint may hang in the air, so it is advisable to wear a mask.

The best motion for spraying is a fluid rotation of the wrist or arm from side to side rather like a steady, featherweight brush-stroke. Keep the spray moving, like a blow lamp, only in wider sweeps; don't keep it pointed at one area or you'll get blotches and – unless you want a mottle – you'll have to respray the whole area. Also, such build-ups of paint can drizzle and stand out badly on the sprayed surface, and are difficult to eradicate if you allow them to coagulate and become viscous.

Sprays are so versatile for softer effects such as distressing and shading that it is tempting to use them beyond their capacity. Do not be tempted to use it on unsuitable surfaces for spraying leaves a surprisingly distinctive effect; it doesn't look good on marbling for instance, being too opaque and powdery. It can give a surface a cardboard appearance, lacking solidity, but for soft transitions and areas of smooth, unruffled colour, spray guns have few equals.

GENERAL PAINTING SEQUENCE

The usual sequence for painting a room is: ceiling, walls, woodwork. When painting walls or ceilings, always paint the edges of sections first – where walls meet each other or a ceiling – using the tip of the brush, and try not to overlap the application into adjacent areas. If you are finishing furniture, it is advisable to do this after the structural elements of the room are complete. This way, you can be certain of matching, or

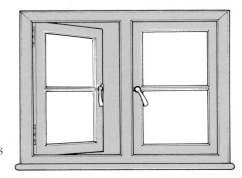

UNORTHODOX EQUIPMENT

Painting tools can be animal, vegetable or mineral. For mottled patterns, such as those found in marble, a sliced cauliflower floret has few equals. Chopped bottle corks make good wood-knot impressions. Cut carrots and potatoes are also useful for all mottled patterns, and crystals on porphyry can be done with diced cabbage, pressed flat by a tin tray. To get whirling paint veins, quarter fill a rubber glove with paint, after piercing the fingertips, and squeeze from the top end. Pencils wrapped in cloth make convincing wood-grain strokes. The most versatile tool of all is your finger: twisted in a cloth to make knots, drawn across a wet glaze for a soft combing effect or in many other ways.

LEFT **Painting sequence for doors and windows** *Starting from the top, paint edges of opening surfaces first, to allow for drying. Paint sills and skirting board last, to avoid picking up dirt from them.*

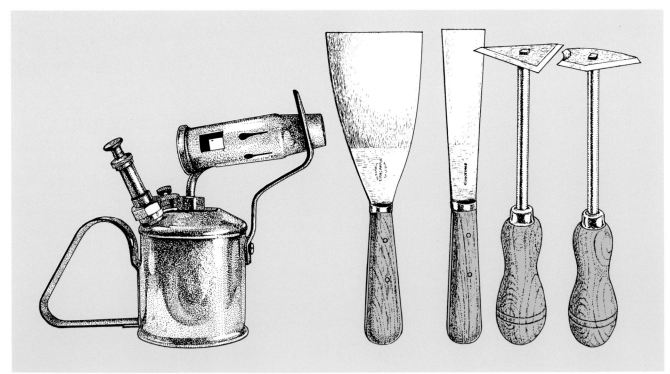

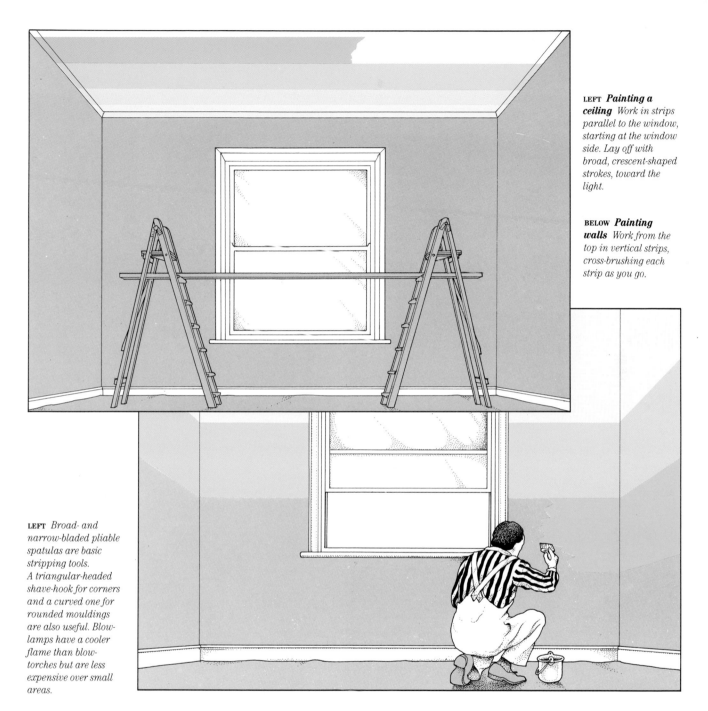

complementing, the main colours of the room, which may alter as they dry.

■ *Ceilings* Start at the window side and work across in 2ft (60cm) strips, parallel to the window. Each strip is best painted in sections 2ft (60cm) square, first laying on strokes parallel to the window, then spreading the paint evenly with broad, crescent-shaped crossing strokes and finally laying off toward the light. Try not to let the strips overlap when brushing on, but cross-brush and

lay off to blend the two wet edges. Don't rush; go briskly but steadily.

■ *Walls* Start at the top-right-hand corner (or left-hand corner if you're left-handed) and work from top to bottom in 2ft (60cm) strips, parallel to the ceiling, cross-brushing each strip into the next as you go and laying off with a light, straight, downward stroke.

■ *Woodwork* Paint the window-frames, picture rail, doors, mantelpiece and

baseboard in that order. This way, the areas that are lightest and cleanest on the brush are done first and the brush is therefore well broken-in but clean (with no loose hairs) before you get to the door – the most noticeable area for flaws, lumps and painterly hiccups. The skirting board comes last because the brush tends to pick up small, unwanted bodies near the floor.

On all woodwork, whether it's a door or a table, laying off strokes should follow the grain.

BASIC ▮▮▮▮▮

PREPARATION

Always strip for action. Take down curtains, pictures and any other easily removable fixtures or fittings that are not to be decorated along with the room. Group furniture in the middle of the room, well away from the wall. For thorough protection, cover both furniture and floor first with plastic sheeting, and then with dustsheets. The plastic will prevent water or paint penetrating through to whatever is underneath, the dustsheet will absorb spills and stop steps or ladders slipping.

Start cleaning by dusting off dry, loose material with either a soft brush or vacuum cleaner attachment, working across the ceiling, down the walls and around and over paintwork, paying special attention to cracks and crevices. Then vacuum the floor so the dust is not spread up the walls or into other rooms.

Ceilings, walls and woodwork that are basically in good condition may only need a thorough cleaning before repainting. Wash off dirt and grime with an old, clean cloth and a bucket containing a solution of warm water and either sugar soap or household detergent. Finish with one or more thorough rinses using clean, warm water and a sponge. Start with the ceiling and work in areas of about 3 sq ft (90 cm^2), taking in the top 6–12 in (15–30 cm) of the walls as you go or, if the room has a picture rail, take in the wall area down to that level. Wash one wall at a time. Don't work from top to bottom: if you start at the bottom and wash up in bands of about 3 ft (90 cm), the water will flow down freely over the wet areas instead of drying out in lines. Catch any remaining dirt by rinsing thoroughly

RIGHT *Planning and patience transform a characterless room into a charming and personal living area (left).*

from top to bottom with clean, warm water while the wall is still wet – and rinse twice if necessary. Wipe off excess water with a clean sponge or chamois leather and allow walls and ceiling to dry completely before starting redecoration.

Painted or varnished woodwork in sound condition should be washed with warm water and detergent, or mineral spirits, to remove dirt and grease, then rubbed down with fine, wet-and-dry abrasive paper to give a tooth to the next coat. (An easy way is to wrap the abrasive paper around a small block of wood such as a child's building brick.) Wipe over with clean, warm water and a rag to remove all traces of detergent and, when thoroughly dry, use a soft, clean, dry brush to dust off any remaining loose material – clean, dry paint-brushes are often useful for this, especially small ones for awkward places. There is no substitute for good preparation, it is time-consuming work but pays dividends in a clean, professional, finished job.

Paint is more versatile than any other surface finish and can be very durable; the animals sketched in earth and resin on the walls of caves have been with us for over 5,000 years. You can ask extraordinary things of paint; one of the few demands it makes in return is that you prepare a surface for it first. Although this may take time, you will be well rewarded if you do it well. So when you think of painting an interior, it's as well to know where it will go easily and where – in the minority of cases – it won't.

You can paint on good paint in good condition, any primed wall in good condition, new plaster and old plaster properly primed, sealed woodwork, sound varnish, lining paper or the backing paper of vinyls, primed fabric, painted or scoured metal, glass and tiles.

You should not paint on peeling paint, crumbling plaster, unsealed plaster, polyurethane varnish or old wallpaper.

You cannot paint on surfaces such as old distemper, unsealed wood, unprepared metal or felt.

Such widely used metaphorical expressions as 'painting over the cracks' and 'doing a whitewash job' are a reminder that paint is only a surface finish. It can cover a multitude of sins but without proper care it can betray them or even make them appear worse.

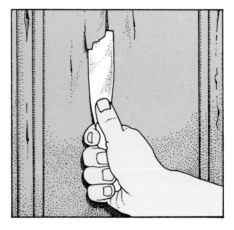

LEFT *Cracking and blistered paint should be tested by running a spatula or stripping knife along the surface behind the paint, keeping the blade as flat as possible. Sometimes no more than this is necessary to remove very thick, dry paint that has shrunk.*

Few things are more depressing in an interior than seeing the joints of old, dried paper as it sags under the weight of new paint, high-gloss paint slapped over window sills with old paint blisters, an acne of trapped dust, unfilled (or, worse, unkilled) wormholes, or little moon-crater chips, all highlighted by the new shiny surface. The preparation of a surface is, thus, very important, do not be tempted to rush this stage.

OLD PAINT

The first thing to remember about paint in interior decoration is that it is not a substitute for structural integrity. If a wall is flaking or a piece of furniture is rotten, it's no good hoping that the paint will glue it together. On a sound surface, however, paint acts as a protective as well as an aesthetic agent. Unless the existing paint is visibly bubbling or peeling, or is damp – which will be betrayed by dark stains like sweat marks (because they actually are sweat marks) or, on light-coloured paint, by yellowish stains like nicotine – it is usually a very good idea to leave the surface untouched, even if you wish to paint over it. Paint applied over sound paint usually retains as good a finish – if not better – as that laid over a stripped surface, and an extra coat only increases the protection.

▮ *Distemper* The absolute exceptions to this are distemper, whiting and lime-wash. These can't easily be over-painted without 'bleeding' or 'dusting into' the new paint on top. They are usually found on older surfaces, particularly in wooden houses or the lower walls of tenement blocks. These surfaces do have to be removed, but fortunately that's quite easy. (After all, the reason you have to take them off is that they tend to come off.) A good way of testing for them if you aren't sure what they look like is to dampen your finger and rub it along the wall: if the paint marks your finger, it is one of the distempers. Distemper may come away similarly on dry fingers, like thin chalk; if that happens, it really has to be taken off.

To remove distemper, whiting or lime-wash, brush vigorously with a dry brush to take off all the dust and 'dandruff' loosely adhering to the surface and then soak the surface thoroughly all over with plenty of warm water, scrubbing with the stiffest scrubbing brush you can obtain. The water will go cloudy very quickly, like thin milk; change it as soon as it does. Rinse the area thoroughly with clean water, and swab it all over with a sponge or soft cloth. You should leave the wall to dry out properly before you put on any type of paint, primer or sealer, or you will get damp underneath the paint.

▮ *Other paints* all other painted surfaces, if they are in good condition, should just be washed down with ordinary soapy water, regardless of what type of paint you intend to put on top. Make sure you remove any grease or

1

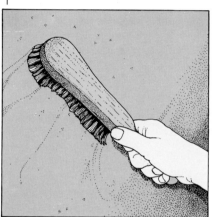

2

3

ABOVE ***Removing distemper***
1 First, brush thoroughly with a dry brush to take off any loose 'dandruff' flakes from the surface.
2 Then thoroughly soak the surface with warm water, rubbing vigorously with the stiffest brush you can obtain. Change the water regularly, as soon as it becomes milky.
3 Once all the distemper has been removed, rinse the surface with clean water and swab it with a sponge or soft cloth.

smudging, crayon or ink from them; ink washes off and things like wax come off with a putty rubber (available from any art shop). Once you've washed the surface with a sponge or cloth, let it dry. Then you can paint on it. When you paint over previous paint, you shouldn't need a primer or sealer because the surface is already sealed. You will in many cases need an undercoat, though, because its prime function is to block off the colour that you are covering up so that it won't show through the top coat.

In the instructions on the back of a can of paint, practically all manufacturers state that loose and flaking paint should be removed before new application. If you do have to remove paint, either from wood or plaster, there are three courses of action open to you. Oil-based paints and latexes are both rather difficult to remove, which is a good reason to leave them there unless they're bubbled, wrinkled or cracked. If the paint is dishevelled in only one or two places, it's better to take it off just from these patches and sand down the edges of the stripped area until they are flush. On wood or plaster, it's best to see if the paint comes off by scraping before you try any other method. Frequently it will, especially if there is a build-up of thick coats and shrinkage has separated them from the surface beneath. Put a knife, a stripping knife or a spatula down behind them, if there's a gap, and run it along the surface, keeping it as flat as possible. If there is no gap, push the knife or spatula into the brittle part of the paint as if you were scraping grease off a plate, again keeping it flat so as not to score the wood or plaster beneath. If the paint comes off, work like this over as much of the area as you can. If other parts obviously ought to go but won't come off this way, then you will have to strip them either by burning or with chemicals. Both these methods can be used on furniture as well as on walls, floors and so forth. Methods of application are the same.

CHEMICALS

Latex paints should generally be removed with chemicals. Chemical paint-and varnish-removers have the advantage of not damaging the surface of plaster or wood, although they can damage clothing and rot shoe-stitching: walk carelessly in their splashes and the soles of your shoes may fall off. They should therefore be used with circumspection for any item involving fabric, such as a chair with an upholstered seat. They are definitely messier than burning-off and they can be more expensive over a large area, too, as you may need more than one application over layered paint. They divide into two types: spirit and alkaline.

Alkaline strippers are very powerful potions and highly effective. They work much more quickly than the spirit type, and are used by industry, professional decorators and artists – sculptors and painters alike – who use them to get special effects. Their strength means that they can be dangerous on the skin and both you and areas not to be stripped must be covered to prevent damage from splashes. They are also more difficult to wash off than spirit-based strippers and, because they are absorbed by wood, they can alter its grain, giving it a raised look. They also rot the hairs of ordinary bristle brushes to a ragged stump. In short, alkaline strippers are very good if you have plenty of experience of them and their properties but for an ordinary domestic interior it's easier and safer to use spirit strippers.

Spirit strippers are normally intended for domestic use, and some are even suitable for use on plastic. Like the more powerful alkalines, they are chemical solvents that soften the paint so that it can be scraped off. Like the alkalines, they are highly toxic, so be sure to work in a well ventilated place. Until recently they were all inflammable, but certain non-flammable brands are now available, which also means it's easier to get rid of the containers.

■ *Tools* A shave-hook, which looks like a trowel at right angles, and a broad-bladed, flat knife are essential for stripping. The best shave-hooks are lozenge-shaped with one straight edge, one curved and one deeply hooked for crannies. Steel wool, toothpicks or sausage sticks and a couple of old (preferably stiff) toothbrushes, one with a broken-off handle and one with a long one, are very useful for details, plaster mouldings or wood. It is advisable to wear rubber gloves, too. The paint stripper should normally be applied with an old paintbrush; even the mildest chemicals will slowly eat brushes. Rags and newspapers are useful, especially for covering floors, and a metal container for collecting paint flakes and scraping tools on is very handy, too.

■ *Application* If you are the type of person who likes to finish a race almost before the starting gun has sounded, chemical strippers are not for you. You do need a considerable degree of patience, not because they're ineffective but because if you wait for them to take effect properly, the actual removal of the paint will be quicker and simpler. In almost all instances, you should brush the stripper on and leave it for at least half an hour. If it is a paste-textured stripper, don't brush it back and forth; put it on in one direction only, because otherwise you'll disturb the film and it won't work properly. Liquid strippers benefit from frequent applications, always keeping the surface wet. In either case, put the first coat on, let it soak in until the paint surface begins to soften, then put a thick second coat on. Then leave it alone. It may take hours to get through a thick build-up of paint – it may even take a couple of days – but that doesn't matter, since, when it has softened right through, the paint can just be stripped straight off like soft pastry, with no hard rubbing, leaving the surface beneath quite bare, clean and undamaged. It really is an awful waste of time and money to rush the job; you'll end up with a tacky, sticky molasses that needs hours and hours of scraping. When you are removing the paint, keep the edge of the tools as clean as possible by scraping them on a can rim or other edge and rubbing them on rags soaked in detergent. Wash the rags and steel wool in detergent, too. When the paint is entirely removed, just wash down the surface with either water or mineral spirits, whichever is the appropriate solvent for the stripper. After the surface has dried you can paint on it, first priming it because it will be absorbent.

BURNING-OFF

Burning-off is generally considered quicker than using chemicals, and can be cheaper. It is much the best way to strip oil-based paints. On thick build-ups it is certainly speedy; on stone or large areas of plaster that are heat-absorbent, not so – and you run the risk of cracking stone. This method is far less messy than using chemicals because the stripped paint is dry and it isn't necessary to cover anything except the area immediately beneath. For a given amount of money, you can strip a similar area with electricity or chemicals, but electricity will be quicker.

There are three types of burner generally available: the new hot-air strippers, blow-torches and the old blow-lamps.
Blow-lamps have been with us for generations and are usually powered by paraffin or petrol. There's nothing wrong with them and if you've got one already there's no need to change it for one of the newer types, although they are more versatile. The shortcomings of blow-lamps are that they have to be constantly refilled, and must be warmed up each time before use; their pressure is variable and they've an irritating habit of suddenly blowing out or flaring.

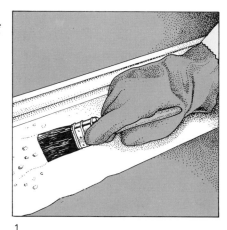

1

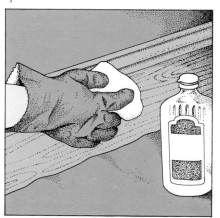

2

3

ABOVE *Application of chemical strippers*
1 Lay liquid stripper on in layers with an old brush, keeping the surface wet until the paint begins to bubble and blister. Then leave the stripper to work.
2 When the paint is putty soft, begin
stripping. Use a pliable, flat blade for flat areas, and a rounded shave-hook for curved mouldings.
3 Clean the surface when the stripping is completed by washing it down with whatever solvent is appropriate to the stripper.

Although their flame is cooler than that of a blow-torch, you sometimes end up setting fire to the paint and burning the surface because of holding the lamp too close to the surface.
Blow-torches are more expensive and therefore are usually hired. They are attached to gas cylinders and have variable nozzles, which means you can adjust the shape of the flame and vary its intensity. Because the flame is hotter than a blow-lamp's, it works faster. It doesn't have to be reloaded and it doesn't blow out. Increased speed may compensate for the expense – it depends what you think your time is worth.
Electric hot-air blowers are the third type of burner. These aren't as new as they're made out to be, and there's a very definite difference between them and the very recent electric strippers that resemble hair-dryers. Hot-air blowers work by blowing air along a flexible hose and over a heater with a variable control in an insulated hand-piece. In many ways these are excellent. They avoid the obvious risk of a naked flame, and unless they are jammed up against wood for a long time they won't scorch it. They also work well on plaster and are excellent for detailed work like mouldings or chair legs.

Be warned about the little electric strippers that resemble hair-dryers. They're adequate for very small, precise details but their heads consist of an electric filament like the one in a light bulb, inside a guard nozzle. This means that they heat a tiny area of paint and are extremely slow. They're fine if you want something to do while planning your will, but try stripping a staircase with one and you'll get an idea of what eternity is all about.

■ *Tools* The tools for burning-off are a flat scraper as wide as the working area will allow, a narrower one, and a shave-hook. You also need to cover the floor. If you are working above bare floorboards, newspaper is quite adequate to catch the paint stripped by a hot-air blower but for the other types of burner aluminium foil is best, as hot slivers of paint will drop constantly. Paint which is melted and scraped off when hot dries and coagulates in hard lumps like plastic ashes and it can stick to rugs and linoleum like toffy. Also useful are a metal container for the shavings, and a bucket of water and some wet sacking in case you do set something alight.

■ *Application* Always work from the bottom up while burning off paint, as the rising heat softens the paint above and makes the work progressively quicker. Aim to heat about a square foot (30 sq cm) at a time but never keep the heat source in one spot – keep it moving constantly to avoid melting and scorching. The aim is to blister the paint, not to melt it into a sticky

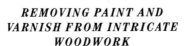

REMOVING PAINT AND VARNISH FROM INTRICATE WOODWORK

Stripping turnings and recesses of wooden furniture is best done with chemicals, as a naked flame can char delicate details if held too close while a scraper picks at them, but the little electric strippers are quite useful for this sort of job. With chemicals, *allow them time to work.* Then, assemble a convenient combination of tools: a small shave-hook (used first to dislodge any lumps); a skewer; a wire-brush; a toothbrush or steel wool. Work down from the top, to avoid sticky bits of paint dropping into crannies already cleaned. You may need three coats of stripper but that's better than scraping too hard at unsoftened paint and damaging the detail. Wash the surface thoroughly when completed, either with a hose and then sponge, or soft brush and sponge. Most varnish removers should be used in the same way but they vary, so read the manufacturers' instructions.

1

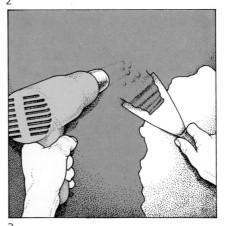

2

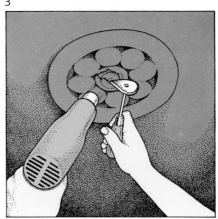

3

4

LEFT **Burning-off paint**
1 Blow-lamps have a cool flame over a small area and the stripping blade should follow closely behind the flame, scraping as soon as the paint blisters.
2 Blow-torches are hotter and can be played over a larger area – about 1ft (30 cm) square – with the blade following upward. They are very fast.
3 Heavy-duty electric hot-air blowers cover large areas with no fire risk, and are effective on oil or latex paints.
4 Little electric strippers with small heating filaments are very useful for close, clean work on precise details, but are far too slow for larger areas.

coagulation that clings to the tools and makes scraping like stirring Christmas pudding. As you move the burner or blower upward, use the scraper behind it, keeping the blade as flat as you can over the surface, so that you won't gouge grooves in it. On wood you can tilt the tool more than on plaster, but not at an angle of more than 15° from the surface, or you'll dig into the grain. Go with the grain if you're stripping wood, *never* across or you'll tear the grain. Move from side to side on plaster. It may sound a bit like trying to conduct an orchestra and signal to traffic at the same time but, in fact, once the knife starts to glide up following the torch it becomes a rhythmical motion and the only real danger is losing concentration. Try to keep to the one-square-foot-at-a-time format because paint that is heated and then not removed coagulates and is harder to get off than before.

PREPARING A PARTIALLY STRIPPED WALL IN GOOD CONDITION

If you have stripped defective paint from a part of a wall and find the rest of the surface quite sound, there's no need to continue removing it. If you find any defects in the plaster where you have stripped the paint, you should fill them. There are a large number of ready-mixed or powder composition fillers available from decorators' and hardware shops, expressly designed for this purpose, and many of them – especially the plastic filler – can be tinted with paint or stainers. If you have decided on the final colour scheme, it is useful to colour the filler accordingly. Fillers tend to be very pale, so if you are going to put dark paint over them it's better to darken them. Once you have filled the area concerned, you should sand it down with a very fine sandpaper, using a gentle circular motion, because paint will show up any ridging mark. If you intend to paint the wall with a water-based paint or latex, you should give the

REMOVING LACQUER AND GLOSS

Gloss paint comes off quite easily either with ordinary chemical strippers or with heat, although flames can make it rather sticky. Lacquer is trickier, and needs specific lacquer removers, usually in two or three applications, applied with a brush. *Do not use heat.* A cabinet-makers' scraper is ideal for removing softened lacquer, and a firm sponge is useful to finish off. Read the manufacturer's instructions carefully, as removers vary.

whole wall surface a coat of primer, otherwise paints like vinyl latex will always show up a filled area as a slightly contrasting patch. If the rest of the wall has gloss paint on it, touch up the filled area with oil-based paint diluted half-and-half with mineral spirits. Allow this to dry, and sand down the edges of the old paint, fill it again and retouch it, and let it dry before you apply the first coat of the new finish. That way you won't get patches under the new surface.

TEXTURED PAINTS

Never was there a clearer exception to the rule 'what goes up must come down'. These 'stone effect' paints compound the removal problem of some latexes because they contain various types of fine to coarse grit; this produces a surface that can be both very attractive and an excellent camouflage for irregularities and cracks, but is virtually impossible to get off. Covering over this surface is not a simple solution either, although cross-lining twice – vertically first, then horizontally – or lining once with linen-backed paper will probably do the trick. If you do try this, it will pay to coat the surface first with old-fashioned, glue-based size, and use a flour-based paste to help it stick. It may be worth sanding it first with a mechanical

sander, but it would help to know the nature of the grit in the paint finish in order to use an abrasive paper that is tough enough for the job. If you are going to attempt to remove the paint completely, try stripping it dry first. The coating is sometimes so close-textured that it forms a skin over the wall rather than bonding to it completely and it may well peel off in strips if a knife is put behind it. Failing this, the next step is to try using a wallpaper steamer to soften the surface sufficiently for stripping. As with wallpaper, work from the bottom up so that the rising steam starts to soften the paint immediately above the area being worked meaning that it will peel off more easily and ultimately make far less work for you. These can be very successful but it is often best to experiment with a friend's or a kettle first.

The last resort – or perhaps the first if there is only a small area to handle – is a new paint stripping compound specially formulated for the job. It's a petroleum-based gel (therefore inflammable, so take the usual precautions) which softens the surface in about an hour. The paint can then be easily stripped off with a knife and the surface washed down with cold water. This chemical remover will also deal with some of the powder-based textured paints – although it may take two coats and will then need a hot-water wash – and the more stubborn of latex paints. The reason for the *caveat* is that it is expensive, but when there's no other alternative, it's probably worth paying the price.

NEW PLASTER

The first thing to be sure of when painting plaster is that it is dry and flat. Of course it should be both, but you can't guarantee that until you look closely (and looking can be full of surprises). Dampness in plaster will give it a slightly piebald effect; the other main concern is that salts and acids may come to the surface under the paint, causing bubbles and cracks. If salts and acids come through water-based latex paint it doesn't really matter, because these paints are porous and the acid and salt appear like fluffy ash and can be brushed off. But if you intend to put on oil-based paint like gloss, flat-oil or eggshell you should put an alkyd-resistant primer on first; this will seal off the acids and salts and stop them making bubbles and 'mole hills'.

As far as the regularity or flatness is concerned, good plaster has a smooth, sheeny surface like cold silk. If it's new it isn't really very hard as yet and it may have little ribs and freckles on it, no bigger than a small mole on your hand. You won't necessarily see these as you look straight at the wall, but paint will reveal them if you don't remove them because they catch the light; they can cause little tail-backs in the paint like tiny tadpoles. To find them, put your face against the plaster and look along the

SAFETY WHEN USING CHEMICALS AND BURNERS

When using chemicals, always wear rubber gloves; they can feel awkward, but are not nearly as uncomfortable as chemical splashes on the skin. If you are working overhead, wear goggles or old polaroid sunglasses, whether using chemicals or flame, and preferably cover your face, too. Use a damp cloth or a proper mask to protect your face from flame, although paper may be an adequate mask near chemicals – provided that you can breathe. With burners, have some wet sacking handy, a stiff-bristled broom, and a metal container for hot peelings. A bucket of water is a good idea, too, with both chemicals and burners. Switch a flame off when you're not using it; if you pause for a short time, turn it right down but with a *visible* flame and stand it well away from any flammable surface.

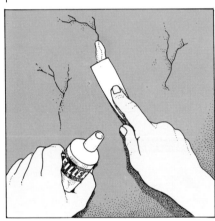

1

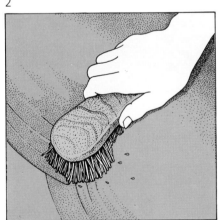

2

3

ABOVE **Painting on new plaster**
1 Pop off any nipples left by the plasterer's trowel or any small flecks stuck to the surface with a broad, flat spatula, keeping the blade as flat to the surface as possible.
2 Fill any cracks and allow them to dry. You can sand the surface of the filler with very fine abrasive paper, but not the plaster. Then prime it.
3 After removing any fine nipples and filling cracks, you can wash the surface down with water and a cloth.

wall towards a light source and, if they're there, you'll see them. To get rid of them, use a 4 in or 5 in (10 cm or 12.5 cm) paint-stripping blade. Slide it flat along the wall and they will pop off: never, never tilt the blade more than a few degrees from the wall or you'll risk digging into the plaster. Absolutely *never* sand plaster that's new and fresh. Even the finest sandpaper will leave little wheeling scratches that will show through three layers of paint, and you'll only have to refill them and paint it all over again. It just isn't worth it.

If you are going to paint plaster with any water-based paint, such as latex, you should give the whole surface a coat of paint mixed half-and-half with water, to seal it. It will look horrible, although it's poetically called a mist or fog coat by many decorators. Its function is to make a bridge or key for the top layer of paint, as much modern paint tends to lie on the surface rather than permeate the plaster, so don't worry about the mottled effect – it's supposed to look like that. This mist coat seals the plaster and stops the top coats going patchy. At this stage, you should fill any small cracks that might have appeared. Use the all-purpose, vinyl-based fillers from decorators' shops that are designed for this. Allow them to dry. You can sand off the filled cracks using a very fine sandpaper once you've sealed the surface around them. Then touch them up with the same half-and-half mixture. If the cracks open a little, just repeat the procedure again, touch it up, let it dry, and you can then think about the finishing coats.

NEW OR NEWLY STRIPPED WOOD

New wood, which has never been painted, should be sanded down all over to remove any small fibrous splinters and also to key the paint. What you want is a surface that feels like smooth peach skin, is really minutely ruffled but has no rough areas that will show up on the

1

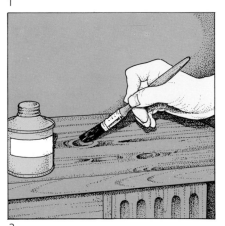

2

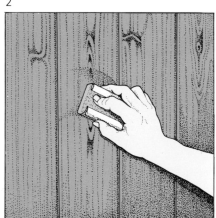

3

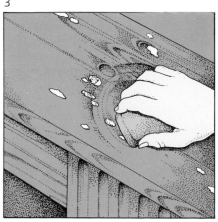

4

RIGHT *Painting on new or newly stripped wood*

1 You can knock out any knots that may cause resin bleeding with a chisel, like coring an apple, and then fill in the holes with plastic filler.

2 Alternatively, give the knots and any resinous areas a coat of good knot sealer; this prevents resin bleeding out.

3 All new wood should be sanded down overall before sealing and priming.

4 Plastic filler is suitable for grooves, cracks and empty knot-holes. Filled sections should always be sanded flush and then sealed before painting.

paint surface. A fine abrasive paper or fine steel wool is quite adequate for this on any planed wood. Most softwoods, especially pine, tend to have resinous knots that can 'bleed' resin rather badly – it looks like corn syrup. If this isn't treated before you paint on the wood there will be sad streaks, like nicotine stains, fretting the paint. There are two things you can do about knots: you can remove them with a chisel, or seal them. On boards you can often knock the knot straight out, as it has no lateral strength, using a chisel and a wooden mallet. If the knot gives downward it should drop out, if not, you'll have to chisel it out like coring an apple. Then you can fill the hole with wood filler. You can paint directly on top of many wood fillers and the plastic fillers and plastic woods can all be primed, in any case. Once you have filled the knot, let it dry and sand it flush with fine sandpaper. You may have to use a number of layers of filler to avoid sinkage in the surface.

If you don't want to try removing the knot, use either an aluminium primer, or knot sealer. Knot sealer is made of pure shellac in wood alcohol. If you use it in a warm room you may feel drunk, and that is not just an illusion – the fumes are intoxicating. Ensure good ventilation. Use two thin coats over the knots and about an inch (2.5 cm) around them. This will stop bleeding.

You must always prime bare wood before you paint on it. Use an aluminium primer on doors and window-frames, as they often come into contact with damp, and especially where wood abuts stone or brickwork. Aluminium primers are also best on any wood with resinous grain – that's an orangey grain that's hard and seems to stand above the softer wood around it. Otherwise, on all bare wood, including furniture, you can use a good, lead-free primer. It is worth stressing here that cheap paint is a waste of money and effort. Always buy the best paint you can afford, and that certainly goes for primers, too.

Combined primer/undercoats have now appeared on the market and they save a lot of time as they make one process unnecessary.

The consistency of the priming coat depends on how absorbent the wood will be. Softwoods – for example, white woods – are very absorbent, and it's useful to add mineral spirits to help the primer to seal the surface. Hardwoods are much less absorbent, and for them the primer needs to be used thick.

On wood that has been stripped but still has traces of paint adhering to it, you have two options for preparation. One is to wet it and then rub it down with a waterproof abrasive paper or pumice stone. Then you should let it dry. Sometimes the grain gets puffy and swells because of the water. This is less common on wood that's been stripped by burning, because the wood has been hardened by the heat and is less absorbent than other bare wood; if it does happen, give the wood a sandpaper rubbing before you prime it. Alternatively, you can use linseed oil and mineral spirits to clean it. Mix one part of the raw linseed oil to three parts of mineral spirits, and rub it in with a pumice stone or self-lubricating paper. Then wash the wood with mineral spirits, rubbing it over with a lint-free cloth. It used to be possible to get painters' tack-rags for this type of job; they were called tack-rags because they were tacky, and picked up all the dust and gritty particles that always manage to get on to surfaces like this. Ironically, as they were so useful, it's now almost impossible to get them, but you can make a fairly effective substitute by cutting a piece of old sheet or shirt – preferably white – and giving it a thorough soaking in warm water, then wringing it out and spreading it flat on a non-absorbent surface. Scatter turpentine over it as evenly as possible, then wring it to get the turps to flow through its fibres evenly. Open it out flat and sprinkle a dessert-spoonful of boat varnish (for a shirt-sized cloth) over it.

1

2

ABOVE **Removal of varnish and wax from wood**
1 Use a cabinet-makers' scraper in conjunction with chemical stripper to remove wax and varnish. To strip wax and leave varnish, give the surface a coat of brass polish and run the scraper over with only moderate pressure.
2 To remove wax and leave varnish over large areas, rub mineral spirits over the whole area with a brush, cloth, steel wool or abrasive paper. In all cases, wash the surface down afterwards with warm, soapy water and allow to dry.

Wring it out again, to spread the varnish all through it, and then hang it up for about 40 minutes. Fold the cloth up into a pad and it will take up just about everything dusty or gritty on the wood surface. This tack-rag will last for many months, provided it is stored somewhere airtight; you can re-treat it if it begins to dry out. Always shake it out after use, or you'll put the muck back on next time.

VARNISHED AND WAXED WOOD

It isn't true that you can't paint over varnish. The glaze technique of oil-painting on gesso or canvas is based on exactly that, but it's not possible to over-paint varnish with water-based paints on plaster or woodwork.

If, for instance, you have a painted surface with crazed varnish (crackling, such as you see on old, glazed tableware), it's quite possible to apply oil-based gloss over this to maintain the cracked effect. You can apply two coats if you want the paint to be more opaque; one, if you want a glossier effect.

If you do decide to strip the surface, the quickest way of removing varnish, dirt and wax is to use a chemical paint and varnish remover. The method is the same as for removing paint, but in place of the shave-hook it's better to use a cabinet-makers' steel scraper.

If you wish to leave varnish on but remove wax, or remove older, softer polish without using the strong chemical paint/varnish removers, you can apply a mildly abrasive brass polish. This will remove wax and leave varnish intact, if you use a cabinet-makers' scraper with a light pressure. To remove the varnish as well, use the scraper more heavily For large areas covered with wax, use mineral spirits and steel wool or abrasive paper. If any residue still adheres, you can take it off with steel wool and benzine. In any case, you should wash the surface down afterwards with warm, soapy water, rinse it thoroughly and allow it to dry.

Shellac and lacquers could, until recently, be removed only with shellac and lacquer thinners, painted on with an old brush – as they destroy the bristles – but a new solvent has become available that will remove both. It won't, however, remove polyurethane varnish – that hard, glassy, general-purpose varnish that comes in matt, silk and hard gloss and seems to be an essential feature of the stripped pine furniture so popular in recent years. Polyurethane can be taken off with chemical paint/varnish remover, applied as above.

PAPER

It's a very common practice for people to slap paint quickly over old wallpaper, but this is usually a mistake. First, once you paint over the paper the paint hardens and makes the paper twice as difficult to get off, should you want to change it. Paint makes wallpaper sticky, ragged and stringy when removed, because you have to break the paint film as well as the paper. Always remember that paint has weight and weight is pulled downwards; so if the paper is not keyed properly the paint will make it sag in places. Also, new paint causes old wallpaper to bleed dye into the paint, so that you get patches that look like distressed leather. The paint also betrays any roughness in the paper surface, and if the paper is fluffy or ragged, you'll get a hairy effect a little like old burlap. All the seams in the paper show up, and the effect can be like an old bed-sheet pinned to the wall after a dose of starch.

Unless the plaster surface underneath is really very dubious and you think it'll be more trouble than it's worth to remove it, you should take paper off a wall before painting. There are very few exceptions to this. One is if the paper is on gypsum block – often found in buildings that have been converted into flats and have rooms or partitions; in this case, you'll have to leave the paper, as it won't come off

1

2

ABOVE **Stripping wallpaper**
1 Sometimes wallpaper will come off dry with a knife. If so, work upward from the bottom, gently and steadily, raising the paper as you insert the knife.
2 If the paper will not come off dry, soak the whole wall with very hot water. Start at the top, as the water runs down and makes the job of saturation quicker.

gypsum block anyway. Also, you may want to retain the texture of a paper. If that is the case, the paper really must be firmly keyed to the wall. If there are any parts that aren't, take them off, and fill the area with vinyl-based filler. Don't on any account size old wallpaper – that's absolutely disastrous; the watery solution makes it swell and bubble and wrinkle and, even if these blemishes settle back and shrink when dry, there will be air bubbles riddling the back of the paper and it will come away from the wall when the paint dries. This can also happen if you put water-thinned, water-based paint on old paper. Either prime the paper or, better still, give it a coat of thin, oil-based paint. The trouble is that some wallpapers bleed colour into the paint, especially red and mauve dyes, which look rather like a bad attack of sunburn. The best thing is to leave the surface for about four days and see what happens. If bleeding starts, give the whole wall or room a coat of knotting diluted with wood alcohol. After that, you should cross-line the walls to hide the joints. Cross-lining is just what it sounds like – putting lining paper across, rather than down, the walls. In all other circumstances, take the paper off if you intend to paint the wall.

Sometimes wallpaper will come off dry with a knife, especially the thick embossed papers and pre-pasted papers. Paper can also be removed with a knife if the wall is very damp or the plaster is crumbly, or if the paper has been steamed off, as it can be in or near a kitchen. It's always worth seeing if it will come off easily. Do this by putting a knife up under a *bottom* corner and then sliding it upward gently, raising the paper and gradually working upward, as if removing a huge sticking plaster. Always work from the bottom up: if you work from the top, the paper will hang down over you as it comes off.

In the majority of cases, however, paper won't come off dry. The most basic method for removing it – and one of the least messy and most effective – is very hot water, the hotter the better. Get a big, flat, 5 in or 6 in (12.5 cm or 15 cm) brush, and soak the whole area – if it's a room, the whole room – thoroughly, several times. *Always do this from the top down:* this way the water runs down and helps soak the paper more thoroughly. Then, using a large flat knife – a spatula is most effective but you can use a large kitchen knife – work downward but with horizontal strokes; paper comes off more easily that way because the resistance of the width of the roll is less than that of its length. Powdered wallpaper strippers can be added to the water, but they don't make much difference to the results.

Most thick build-ups of paper come off better by steaming than by hot water alone. You can get away with using a bevy of electric kettles in a small room, if you have enough of them; line them up along the wall to create a small sauna and work *from the bottom up,* because heat rises. Over large areas of thick, intractable paper, getting a steam stripper is probably the best policy. Steamers work on almost all papers, and you can hire them. They have a perforated plate like the rose on a watering-can, at one end of a long hose; the steam is passed up the hose from a tank of water heated by electricity or by

SHADING A CEILING

This can be done from the centre outward, or across diagonally. If you are working from the centre mix the centre tone and those at the corners first, then the intermediate tones. One person should do the centre and another the corners, simultaneously; the intermediate tones should then be added by one person, and blended by the other. Oil-based paint is best; latex is unsuitable, as it dries so quickly. When shading diagonally, use the method recommended for walls.

a gas cylinder. You hold the steam plate against the paper for about half a minute. This softens the paste and allows the heat to travel upward. Don't hold it longer than that in one spot or you'll run the risk of bulging the plaster. Run the knife upward and across from the bottom of the wall. The only paper that can resist a steam stripper is – predictably – the varnished paper of eighty years ago, which still lurks under others in bedrooms and hallways. On good old-fashioned principles, this paper was built to last and last it certainly does. It's probably under there because no one else could get it off before you. The best approach is to score it carefully – to let the steam penetrate – and then try a kettle nozzle right up against it. If it surrenders and your knife starts to lift it, well and good. If it doesn't then it's going to resist to the bitter end, so don't waste your time trying to steam it off: you won't be able to. You will have to cover it with another medium.

Paper that has already been coated with latex or any other water-based paint will usually need steaming. Heavily embossed papers may need it if they've been painted, but if you scrub at the raised areas with a wire brush they usually come away. Vinyls can often be lifted dry by the bottom corner of each panel but the backing paper often remains stuck to the wall – you will have to remove that by the methods described above, although if it's very flat and firmly stuck you can paint over it.

The most difficult of the modern papers to remove are the washable ones, because they have been waterproofed by the manufacturers to avoid their being steamed off inadvertently. They are also thin and filmy. As with varnished paper, you have to score them to let the steam penetrate; but unlike the varnished papers, they will then come off with conventional soaking and scraping.

Once you have removed any of these papers preparatory to painting, wash the wall down thoroughly to remove all the old paste or size and leave it to dry.

1

2

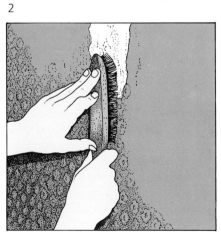

3

ABOVE *Using a steamer*
1 Hold the steam plate to the paper for about half a minute but no longer, as prolonged use may cause wall plaster to bulge. Work from the bottom up, as heat rises.
2 Score embossed paper with a sharp knife to allow the steam to penetrate.
3 Scrub thick papers before steaming, this causes gaps for the heat to penetrate;

Then sand it down with abrasive paper and dust it off. After that you can prime it.

HARD COVERINGS

The main problem with any hard covering is not so much the material itself as the adhesive – the better it sticks, the harder it is to unstick. Even the professionals can find it impossible to decide, simply by looking, just what type of adhesive has been used for the job. In any case, the enormous range and complex make-up of modern adhesives means that it is usually neither time- nor cost-effective to try to find the appropriate solvent. Even if you find it, trying to remove the adhesive with a solvent is a messy job; the solvent will penetrate the surface, which in turn can mean a lengthy cleaning and sealing operation. In most cases, therefore, it is advisable to try removing hard coverings and their adhesives dry and just resign yourself to the fact that it may be a tedious job. The condition of the wall will also have to be taken into account. Some adhesives are so strong that the plaster will also be pulled off and you may have to replaster or at least re-skim. So, before attacking the old surface, do consider whether there is any other acceptable method of covering it up.

The tools that are likely to be needed for dry stripping are a hammer, chisel, broad knife, craft knife, various grades of abrasive paper and a sanding block. Punch ceramic tiles off the wall with a hammer and chisel first, using the stripper to scrape away any remaining adhesive. With more flexible hard coverings rubbery strings of adhesive may be found, connecting wall to covering as you start to pull it away. Use the craft knife to sever these strings as close to the background surface as possible. In all cases, once the covering is off, punch away as much of the remaining adhesive as possible with the stripper, trying not to damage the surface, sand off the rest and dust.

Adhesive manufacturers are well aware that, in solving some of the problems, they have created others and are themselves experimenting with various methods of adhesive removal. This is very much at the 'trial and error' stage, but it is worth reporting their findings so far, in case dry stripping does not work and you find yourself, quite literally, stuck. The most successful method to date appears to be the wallpaper steam stripper, particularly in softening the standard, ready mixed PVA adhesives often used to stick ceramic tiles and expanded polystyrene ceiling tiles. They will still neeed punching off first to allow the steam to reach the adhesive and, with porous surfaces like plaster, be prepared for a thin film of the surface to come away with the adhesive as you scrape it off. If you're proposing, therefore, to re-cover with a heavy cladding, bind the wall first with a PVA bonding agent, diluted according to the covering – for example, 1:5 with water for a heavyish wallpaper, but undiluted for ceramic tiles, and make sure that you put the tiles up with the recommended adhesive while the bonding surface is still tacky, otherwise they may well not stick securely.

The steamer is less successful with the rubbery types of adhesive, particularly if there's a hard, impervious surface behind it. However, good reports

have been received about using a hot-air stripper on this type of adhesive. Burning it off is another possibility, provided it is not cellulose-based and therefore likely to catch fire. But test a small and preferably isolated area first to check the behaviour of the adhesive and whether it is likely to give off unpleasant and possibly toxic fumes, as this can be dangerous and, anyway, is unpleasant. So be warned and take the extra time to test first.

FABRIC

If a wall or piece of furniture is covered in burlap, canvas, linen or jute, you can paint on it if you want its texture; there's no need to remove it. Artists paint on canvas as a matter of course. Expensive fabrics like silk cannot be sealed, so they are unsuitable for painting on. Silk will become soggy in patches and, if it dries out, will be brittle. Felt is also unsuitable for over-painting, as its texture is too hairy to take paint well.

If you want to use a water-based paint like latex, all you have to do is prime the fabric with a thinned coat or two. Then allow it to dry before putting on two coats of normal consistency. Before using oil-based paints you will need to apply a warm, weak solution of size, to penetrate the fabric weave and stop it going brittle. You should let this dry – you can tell when it is dry as it lightens in colour and feels dry – before you put on a primer and then a finishing coat. The drying times may vary according to the fabric, but follow the drying times stated by the manufacturer and allow a bit over just to be on the safe side.

Canvas can take almost any type of paint, provided that it is properly primed. Only water-colours (as distinct from water-based acrylics) are inappropriate to it, as their texture is too delicate for its weave. Canvas on a wall or modern chair is usually pre-stretched; that is it is already taut. Any paint finish that is already on it can be

ABOVE *Proper planning will prevent nasty surprises once your fond imaginings have become all too real, and perhaps, irredeemable. Make sample boards to assess whether colours, textures and patterns will work together. This is a remarkably accurate halfway stage between the conception and reality of a room and is an invaluable aid to ensure that what you see in your mind's eye is what you get.*

RIGHT *With the use of colour samples the finished room successfully resembles the initial idea, and no element overpowers another, or is at odds with the total design.*

PAINT ON METAL FURNITURE

Most domestic metal-framed furniture is tubular stainless steel and cannot be painted. However, some older cast-iron garden furniture may have found its way inside the house, and provided any rust is first removed you can paint it. Prime it with metal primer/sealer, then apply two coats of oil-based gloss paint, *never* water-based. Wrought iron requires its own special paint, obtainable from ironmongers.

painted straight over although, if it is a darker colour than the intended top coat, it may need a preparatory coat. Fabric on soft furnishings must be stretched taut before painting.

CANVAS ON FURNISHINGS

New canvas, if it is to be applied to a furnishing such as a screen, needs to be primed and stretched – which actually means shrunk – on to a frame or stretcher. This wooden frame should be constructed so that it has enough lateral strength to resist the strong pull of the canvas (a yacht's tubular steel mast will buckle before its canvas splits) and, if the frame is larger than 3 ft × 4 ft (90 cm × 120 cm), it should have at least one lateral cross-piece at the centre. A sheet of linen- or cotton-duck canvas should be cut by laying the frame on the sheet and using a pair of scissors or a sharp craft knife to cut round the frame, leaving at least 3 in (7.5 cm) to allow enough canvas to be bent over the edges of the frame. Then, beginning at the centre point of each side in turn, and working up to the corners simultaneously (not doing just one side first), either staple or tack the canvas on to the stretcher. Use rust-proof, bayonet-type, flat-headed tacks if possible, pulling the cloth as tight as you can, and making sure that the weave isn't stretched across the frame diagonally, but is square.

The corners should be folded last, in the same manner as folding the corner of a sheet under a mattress, and then pinned or stapled. The canvas at this stage should be taut, but not too tight. You should then prime the canvas with acrylic or oil-based primers, preferably with two coats. For this size, artists' primers are best. Acrylic primers dry quickly. Priming can be done with an ordinary decorators' brush, loading the bristles liberally. Do not scrub the surface, but work the primer well in with a cross-hatching movement. Coat the fabric so that the little holes in the

weave show little blobs of paint if you look at the back of the canvas. As the primer dries, the canvas will shrink until it becomes drum-tight. After about 24 hours you should sand it over with very fine abrasive paper, with a quick, light circular motion, and give it another coat of diluted primer.

METAL

The types of metal usually met with in domestic interiors are not easy to paint; most common are galvanized steel – window-frames and radiators – copper piping and chrome furniture.

Window-frames are rustproofed before fitting, and that makes the keying of paint very difficult on any of the older ones from the 1930s to the 60s and, with the exception of some recent models that allow for painting, they are basically greasy when new and never intended for paint. The most common approach to painting sound, unrusted, galvanized steel is to wash it in mineral spirits and then in mordant. You have to clean it in such a way that the undercoat you use will key to the metal, and mordant – a chemical etching solution – will do this. After the mordant is applied, the metal should be washed thoroughly with water and left to dry, with no loose material being left on it. There are very good zinc chromate primers available, which also protect metal against rust, but unfortunately a lot of undercoats don't key to them. The only way around this is to read the manufacturers' recommendations very carefully.

Any attempt to paint over rusted metal is absolute folly and doomed to failure. You have to remove any rust before you can attempt to paint the surface. It depends if the metal is lightly or heavily rusted. Light rust looks like a pocky powder on the surface, and against this chemical rust removers are adequate but they have to be cleaned off very thoroughly or they make the subsequent application of paint very

44

difficult. Tedious as it is, there is no real substitute for chipping and scraping to remove heavy rust. There is no special combination of tools for this: any scrapers, blunt chisels, spatulas, knives, wire brushes, abrasive paper or steel wool can be used – preferably the scrapers first, then the brushes, then the wool. Just keep on going until you work down to a bare, clean surface. That's all there is to it – and you'll probably think that's quite enough. There's no quick way of doing it if you're going to do it properly. You will also need thick gloves: gardening gloves or motorcycle gauntlets are very effective skin-preservers.

Radiators are commonly pre-finished in enamel, but this can chip and become grubby or rusty. So, if necessary, strip the paint. The best method is to use a chemical stripper and then to clean the rust, if any, off the bare metal. It is best to get the radiator hand-hot if you intend to paint it, and then to prime it with zinc chromate while it's warm. Whatever you do, *don't* apply a water-based paint to a radiator, because it will rust. Always use an oil-based paint. There are now special heat-resistant paints that can be applied to warm, dry, clean metal – but it must be all of those things. It is worth noting that gloss paints do not conduct heat as well as flat oil-based paints, because of their surface skin. All colours will ultimately fade on a heated surface but darker colours alter more than light ones.

Copper and chrome should never be painted. Paint simply doesn't stick well and flakes when heated. Even if you rub copper down with emery cloth and mineral spirits, you can't rub it dry; you have to let it dry of its own accord because copper dust floats and then leaves blue-green speckles like lichen wherever it falls. Copper always gets its revenge for the outrage of being painted, but if you really feel you have to, prime it with zinc chromate and then apply gloss paint directly to that with no undercoat. It won't last any length of

time but it will outlast other methods; the copper will always win in the end. As both copper and chrome are really very handsome metals if left unmolested, why not just polish them and enjoy them as they are?

TILES

Tiles, if they have never been painted before, need only be washed down with detergent to remove any grease and then left to dry. There are some excellent brands of paint on the market expressly intended for tiles, their only drawback being that the colour range is somewhat limited, as they are intended primarily for flooring; however, you can always mix them. There is also a wide range of enamel paints – from those used on boats to those used on model aeroplanes – which work very well on tiles and don't need an undercoat. If the surface is already painted and in good condition, you can paint straight on it. Latex and water-based paints are not at all suitable for tiles, as they tend to flake. In any case, painting tiles with that type of paint rather defeats the point of having them.

To clean paint from tiles, if necessary, it's easier to use a chemical stripper in the usual way. Do not attempt to burn off old paint; you run the risk of cracking the tiles, and they will absorb the heat.

REMOVING OLD DISTEMPER

If distemper marks your fingers when rubbed, it will usually come off with a stiff brush. Whether or not it comes off to the touch, brush it vigorously with a hard brush, then soak the surface with warm water and scrub it hard, changing the water as soon as it becomes milky. Then wash it down thoroughly with a sponge, allow it to dry, and prime it before painting.

RIGHT *Filling the pits and inevitable cracks which occur in plaster (after some years) can take quite a while. When removed, wallpaper may leave an acne of freckles on the plaster beneath. Plaster shrinkage from skirting boards may leave lines of little holes. To ignore any of these problems will mar the final painted finish. Corners, in particular, catch the light and should be pointed up sharply. The main thing to remember is that preparation takes longer than application of the finish, but it's worth doing properly. The paint will last far longer and look infinitely superior on a well-prepared surface, giving a far more professional appearance.*

BROKEN
COLOR

Broken colour means applying one or more colours in broken layers over a different-coloured background. This approach makes the most of paint's great versatility, and the variety of effect is equalled by the simplicity and effectiveness of the method. The results almost always give a unique one-off finish and offer wide-ranging options to those who feel that plainly painted walls look bleak, but cannot find or afford the paper or pictures they might prefer.

Techniques of broken colour date right back to the Ancient Egyptians and the same methods are practised all over the world. Professional decorators, however, have taken care that their methods remain secret, as most are so simple to apply that in many cases amateurs can use them just as

effectively themselves. These techniques vary in visual texture and depth as well as colour and they have a very practical advantage: they can disguise the superficial imperfections of a surface by utilizing them as part of the process.

All broken colour-effects divide into two basic types: those where you add paint and those where you remove it. Where you add paint, as in spattering or sponging, you can use a wider range of materials; for example, you might use water-based latex paint and flat-oil paint, eggshell and glaze, all on the same area. On the other hand, with the subtractive techniques, such as combing or stippling, there is less scope because you need a slow-drying paint that will stay wet, and therefore workable, longer. This means that the quick-drying, water-based latexes are more difficult to use than oil-based paint but you can use them to achieve a different type of finish with the same method.

Because latexes don't need an undercoat, you can keep them workable longer by applying a coat of the more slow-drying, silk-finish paints first and then applying the latex on top. The latex will then soak into the area beneath more slowly and stay workable longer. Latex has a softer effect than oil-based paint if you use it for ragging, combing, dragging or stippling, producing a range of cloudy effects from distressed leather to thin cotton. The oil-based paints give a sharper finish which, in combing and stippling, is rather more sophisticated. The general principle is to use flat, oil-

LEFT *This light ochre wash gives both warmth and lightness to a high room. While setting the basic colour tone, it allows great freedom to the rest of the decor.*

RIGHT *The contrast of matt wash to sharp, white woodwork accents the proportions of the room and allows the furnishings a clean, mellow backdrop which accords with their quiet warmth and weight.*

based glaze over flat-oil paint, eggshell
or undercoat, and a water-based glaze or
wash over latex. A latex ground needs no
undercoat – although it's best to put two
coats on new plaster – but always be
sure that the ground coat is grease-free
or the decorative top coat won't take
properly. If you are going to use oil-
based paint on new plaster, put a
primer/sealer on, then an undercoat and
a low-lustre eggshell as a ground coat.
It's worth repeating here that three or
four thinned coats are preferable to one
thick one. It's essential to let the ground
dry out completely before glazing or
applying another decorative top coat.

MIXING AND THINNING

One of the economic advantages of these
finishes is that the top coats are always
thinned so that you generally only need
between one-third and one-half the
quantity of paint normally required for
the room. Thinning is important, first for
reasons of workability, and second for
effect – the desired texture comes from
the broken nature of the colour, not
from three-dimensional splotches of
paint or glaze. The thinner the paint or
glaze, the lighter and/or more
translucent the effect, but obviously
beyond a certain level of thinning the
preparation becomes too runny and so
unworkable.

■ *Latex paint* should be thinned with
water – about one part paint to three
parts water. Make it four parts water for
greater translucency but, depending on
the paint, you may find it runs too much
and that more paint is needed to make it
more workable.

■ *Flat oil paint, undercoat or eggshell*
should be thinned with mineral spirits
(the solvent sometimes called
turpentine substitute). Start with a half-
and-half mixture of paint and solvent,
adding more solvent, a little at a time,
until the desired consistency is reached.
If, on testing, the mix is too liquid to

hold the effect you're using, add either
some more paint or a little proprietary
drier: usually up to a tablespoonful per
quart/litre of thinned paint will do the
trick, but don't add too much or the
finish may dry to a brittle surface.

■ *Oil-based paint and glaze,* thinned
at least half-and-half with mineral
spirits, is a mixture used by some
decorators. This makes a very workable
formula which holds out well (adding
more glaze will make it less opaque and
it will stay workable even longer), but
the paint in the mixture can start to
separate after a while, so don't mix up
more than you can use in a day.

■ *Glaze* gives the most glowingly
translucent of broken finishes. As
the proprietary glazes vary in
consistency, start by thinning half and
half with mineral spirits. You will still
get a workable consistency if you double
the amount of solvent, but just bear in
mind that the more solvent you add, the
quicker the glaze will dry; so take care
before over-doing the solvent.

COLOUR-WASHING

For return on time, effort and money
invested, colour-washing comes high on
the list of decorative wall finishes. When
properly applied on a sound, dry, well-
prepared wall, a tinted wash can give
the surface a perfect matt finish, rather
like the texture of blotting paper yet
with a very unprosaic, almost luminous
quality. The translucent nature of this
medium is particularly useful where the
walls require a glow – perhaps to warm
up a north-facing room with yellow
ochre or deep rose, without the
dominance those colours would have if
used solid in neat paint form. Although a
colour-wash effect is often considered
more suited to country-style rooms of
pine and wicker furniture, coir matting
and cotton prints, it can easily take
much more adventurous applications.
For example, in Paris, one of the top

LEFT *In this marbled hall it is the translucency of one thin coat of colour over another and another which builds up the surface and gives it depth and a kind of stylized realism.*

interior designers 'dirtied' and aged his white wall with a buff wash as an absolutely stunning foil to his collection of classic modern furniture. In this case, the wash was the merest film of water colour, but the texture of a wash can vary, depending on consistency and application, from translucent to near-opaque and from even to rough, the latter being a particularly sympathetic ally to uneven walls – a useful tip for those who are despairing at the state of their walls.

DISTEMPER

Colour-washes also have the advantage of being cheap. The traditional and perfect material for this technique was distemper, and although you can no longer buy distemper in Britain (it is still available in certain parts of Europe), it is easy enough to make. You need whiting (basically crushed chalk – powdered, washed and dried); glue size (the kind containing alum will help bind the distemper and prevent mould, but it is insoluble and therefore harder to remove when you want to redecorate); a tinting agent such as artists' acrylic, gouache or powder colours, or decorators' universal stainers; water and two buckets. Make the distemper by breaking up the whiting into smallish lumps in a clean bucket and covering it with cold water. Leave the whiting to soak for about 30 minutes before pouring off any excess water and beating it into a smooth, thick batter. Mix the size according to the manufacturers' instructions with hot water and blend it with the whiting knife while it is still in its warm, liquid state. Whichever kind of stainer you use, mix it thoroughly into a solution with cold water first; if it is added dry it is unlikely to disperse evenly and will produce unwanted streaks of pure pigment on the wall.

Since distemper lightens considerably as it dries, you may want to test the colour first. In this case, mix the stainer thoroughly into the whiting – a little at a time, more can always be added, but not taken away – and brush a sample on to a piece of lining paper, drying it on a sunny window-sill or in front of the fire (otherwise you will not get a true impression of the colour, as size tends to darken when it is artificially dried). Once you have reached the colour you want, add the size. If for any reason the size was mixed in advance and has set to a jelly, heat it up in its bowl over a container of water on the stove. How much size to add is a delicate business and just about impossible to specify on paper. Size is the binder for the distemper – without it the distemper would dry as a loose powder that would simply rub off as soon as it was touched, but if too much size is added, the distemper could come off in flakes. The trick is to add a little of the runny size at a time, mixing thoroughly and allowing it to cool and thicken the distemper until it reaches the consistency of standard emulsion paint. Use it in this consistency for the full covering power of a ground coat, but for a superficial wash coat, thin it to a milky consistency with water. Either way mix only as much distemper as you can use in a couple of days before it starts to go off.

■ **Preparation** Distemper can be applied on any sound, dry, flat finish except on top of old distemper, where it will produce a patchy result due to the old ground colour 'pilling' as the new is brushed on. Wash off any old distemper thoroughly and prepare the walls for the new coat with either a coat of pure size or claircolle – a straight mixture of size and whiting, which will give a uniformly porous white base coat and make a good ground for the first coat of tinted distemper.

■ **Application** The only problem with distemper, as with any water-based paint, is the speed with which it dries. This makes it harder to keep a wet edge going and avoid hard lines. Adding a small amount of glycerine – about one

RIGHT *On mid-grey, rough-textured walls an ultra-thin wash of charcoal breaks up the ground colour and emphasizes the texture as it nestles in dips and hollows, and intensifies the natural effect of light and shade.*

tablespoonful per quart/litre (theatrical scene painters sometimes use molasses) – will help slow down the drying process, as will keeping doors and windows closed while work is in progress. Apply the distemper liberally and quickly, starting on the window side of the room and working away from it. Make your last 'laying off' brush strokes towards the light to minimize the chance of the strokes being visible and try not to miss out sections, as it's hard to touch up distemper without it showing. If you do miss a patch, it is probably better to sponge the colour on to the bare area, rather than risk an odd, obvious brush stroke. Once the work is finished, it should be dried as quickly as possible, so throw doors and windows open and, if it's a ground coat, leave it to dry for a good 24 hours before adding the final, wash coat of thinned distemper.

OTHER TYPES OF WASH

There are one or two modern alternatives to distemper and choice depends on the effect you want to achieve. For an all-over, near-matt finish of translucent colour, try well-thinned,

RIGHT *It can take courage to use a colour wash – to adjust and accept its naturally unfinished appearance. In this cottage bedroom, the condition of the surface has been* *visually intensified – thick white distemper washed with an almost translucent buff to 'age' it authentically, deliberate 'damp spots' and the floor patchily stained to match.*

flat oil paint (about one part paint to seven or eight parts mineral spirits) over an eggshell ground. If the work is done reasonably quickly, the wash will stay 'open' long enough for you to avoid hard edges and work out brush marks. If, on the other hand, you actually want to get the 'distressed' and textured effect of criss-crossing brush marks, you can simply achieve it by using latex paint, thinned with water. The most

colours in water or solvent and mixing this solution with the undiluted paint before thinning. The importance of mixing thoroughly cannot be stressed too strongly; the tiniest speck of pure pigment can become a huge dark streak across a wall.

■ *Preparation* With the exception of the flat oil version, the washes mentioned above should be applied on to a flat, latex-painted surface: the flatter and more absorbent the ground, the easier it is to apply these very liquid washes over the top. But the surface must be absolutely clean and free of grease, or the wash will simply run off any of these patches. To check that all grease has been removed after washing, wipe the wall over with a solution of warm water and vinegar, rinse thoroughly and leave it to dry completely before applying the colour-wash. Cover the floor with plenty of absorbent, protective layers and keep newspaper and/or rags handy for mopping up.

■ *Method* Slap the colour-wash on liberally and loosely, brushing in all directions and trying to keep a wet edge going as well as avoiding any heavy brush marks. If you want an open, more 'distressed' texture, deliberately leave some areas of ground colour showing through on this first coat, or just skim some parts very lightly with the brush. Be prepared for this first coat to look awful, and wait until it is quite dry – about 24 hours – before applying a second. Distribute this second coat more evenly, so that it covers any previously unpainted parts as well as enriching the colour in the already painted areas. Work as quickly and loosely as possible, especially if you are adding one or more darker tones of wash for a richer effect. If the wash starts running down the walls, don't panic, work it in vigorously with a soft, dry brush and/or add a little more latex paint to the wash and use a sponge to fill any bare patches.

ABOVE *A thin, 'brushy' wash of salmon pink over cream softens the salmon and gives the whole surface a peachy bloom. On the left, a similar consistency of wash in corn over a cream ground produces a patchy effect which* *suits the random collection of earth-toned and metal objets. In both cases, the naturally rough nature of this finish is crisped out of tattiness by the fresh, sharp angles (top) and plans of white-painted woodwork.*

translucent of washes is made from pure pigment and water, with a very small amount of latex added just to give the mixture some body and make it more brushable. The quantities of colour/water/latex will vary according to the desired richness of the finish, but in general, use about two tablespoonfuls of paint per quart/litre of water. For the colour, start with one small tube of gouache (it is expensive, but a little goes a long way), adding more if necessary. Whatever you're mixing, follow the same sequence of dissolving

❚ *Finishing* The intermediate stages of colour-washing can be rather a heart-stopping process, but it is unbelievable how well a couple of coats blend together when dry – and how different and much more 'deliberate' it will look once you have sharpened up the room's edges by repainting doors, windows and skirting boards. Colour-washed walls tend to look best if they are left in their matt, rough, rather unfinished-looking state, but if you feel the finish must be protected – for example, you may want to wash the walls, although this kind of 'open colour' effect seems to survive dust and dirt with more resilience – use clear, matt polyurethane varnish. Just be prepared for the slight sheen effect that even the mattest of varnishes will give.

SHADING

The blending of one colour into another across a wall or ceiling not only looks attractive, it can also visually affect the proportions of a room in a much more subtle way than flat colour. In a high-ceilinged room, cream shading up the walls into buff, and the same buff covering the ceiling would be a much more sophisticated way of visually 'lowering' the ceiling than simply painting the walls cream and the ceiling buff. The same trick used in reverse would imperceptibly 'lift' a low ceiling. Shading walls in panels from a light centre to dark perimeter can also be very effective and shading need not only be in the various tones of the same colour; harmonizing tones of different colours can work well together, but the choice and sequence of colour is crucial, otherwise, for example, by placing opposing colours next to each other you may end up with 'dirty' neutrals or dark bands between the two. Try shading blush pink into a delicate blue-green, for instance, and the area of overlap will turn a murky grey, whereas moving from pink through lilac to mauve would be a smooth and pleasing transition.

Although shading in tones of one colour can happily accommodate fairly dramatic shifts from light to dark, shading with more than one colour generally works best in the lighter, pastel shades. This advice may be erring on the side of safety, but if you really want to try shading a wall from, say, yellow ochre through flaming orange to bright scarlet or crimson, just remember that you will also have to live with it!

OIL-BASED PAINT

❚ *Materials* Flat-oil paint is undoubtedly the easiest material to use for shading, but nowadays it is generally only obtainable through specialist suppliers and in a very limited range of colours. Undercoat makes a reasonably satisfactory alternative, is easy to apply and can be bought anywhere. Whichever you choose, it is more economic to buy it in a large can, either white or something near the palest of a set of toning colours, and tint it yourself to the exact shades required. As usual with oil-based paints, mix the pigment – universal stainer or artists' oil-colours – to solution form with a little mineral spirits before adding to the paint; add them gradually – they can colour up the paint quicker than you'd expect – and stir well to avoid streaking. You will find the paint easier to both apply and blend if you thin it with mineral spirits first, but in this case don't thin more than one part mineral spirits to three parts paint because you need to retain the covering power of the paint to achieve the most even and effective finish.

❚ *Tools* Ordinary paintbrushes are required for applying the ground coat and for applying and rough-blending the top coat, but the final blending needs to be done with a stippling brush. These are expensive to buy, but there are more economical stippling-tool alternatives. Ordinary household items such as bunched-up rags and sponges may be used.

▮ *Ground* Always undercoat for flat oil paint and apply enough top coats of paint, in the lightest of your shading colours, to give a solid finish. Thinning the last of these coats a little with 1:2 mixture of linseed oil and mineral spirits will give it just enough gloss when dry to help you manipulate the shading coat. If there is to be much difference in the tone of the shading colours – for example, shading from *eau-de-Nil* through to deep turquoise – roughly blend the last ground coat, too, to stop the lightest colour grinning through the darkest.

▮ *Tones for the top coat* On normal-sized walls, three shades of colour should be adequate, so tint up the lightest and darkest colours first and then mix some of each colour together to form a middle tone. For very large or, especially, very high walls you may need to make up five, carefully graduated tones by mixing some of the middle one first with the lightest and then the darkest. Apart from careful colouring, the other important requirements is that the paint stays 'open' long enough for you to work on it. As thinning the paint with mineral spirits will only encourage it to dry more quickly, the process can be slowed down by adding some clear oil glaze to the paint (about one part glaze to eight parts paint) if you are dealing with relatively small patches. For very large areas, add about the same amount of raw linseed oil.

▮ *Method* Whether working in bands or panels, accuracy will be helped if the wall is divided up by snapping a chalk-line across and/or down the point at which the move from one colour into the next occurs. (You can buy self-chalking lines, which are very convenient, but for a one-shot job you might just as well make your own with twine and pale blue chalk, using a spirit level and plumb to get lines horizontal and vertical.) Whichever direction the shading is to take, apply the lightest colour first, then

the second colour, working it into the first and blending the two together with the paintbrush. If this is all left to the stippler, the colours will merge too suddenly instead of the ideal, almost imperceptibly graduated blend. Apply subsequent bands of colour in the same way, brush-blending each into the previous one and use all colours liberally – they must stay wet for as long as possible so that the final blending can be done easily with the stippling brush. Once all the bands of colour are brushed on, start stippling from light to dark, working gradually and evenly from band to band of colour. If possible, change stippling brushes half way to avoid taking too much of the lighter colour into the dark, or at least quickly rinse out the stippling brush in mineral spirits and dry it off before moving on. It will help speed up the process if you can enlist another pair of hands, so that one person can paint while the other starts

ABOVE *Shading offers a delicacy and ambiguity of light to wall and ceiling areas of almost any size. Depending on whether the room is used, throughout the day or only at certain times, the colour shift can be used to achieve a dramatic effect in strong sunlight or bright artificial light or gentler effects in softer light. Remember that natural light shouldn't contradict the direction of the shading, or you'll lose the transition altogether.*

stippling. But only one person should do the stippling work, as touch varies from one individual to another and will inevitably show up in the finished surface.

WATER-BASED PAINT

This is a much dicier business than shading with oil paints, mainly because a water base encourages quicker drying, by evaporation rather than reaction, and so it is much harder to keep the wet edge that you need for successful blending. If you are going to attempt it, use a 'silk finish' paint to give a less-absorbent ground coat. Before starting work on the shading, create as damp an atmosphere as possible, by shutting all doors and windows and sprinkling or spraying the floor with water, if you can do so without damaging it, or laying down dampened dustsheets over plastic sheeting. If you are painting on a lining paper, wet it thoroughly with a brush and clean water before starting to paint. Work in narrow bands of colour, starting with the lightest and adding a little more of the dark tone to it as you move from band to band. Brush and stipple between each band as you go. In this way you should be able to keep a wet edge 'alive' between bands. Although the lining paper will blister because it is so wet, it should shrink back satisfactorily as it dries, as long as it is well stuck to the wall. Chances of success with water-paint shading will be increased if you stick to smaller areas and it will greatly help if you satisfy some of the porosity of the wall by coating with an oil primer first.

SPONGING

Sponging is probably the quickest and easiest of all the broken colour techniques mentioned here, largely because – unlike most of the others – it is being used to put paint on the ground rather than take it off. This makes the technique easier to control and there is

1

2

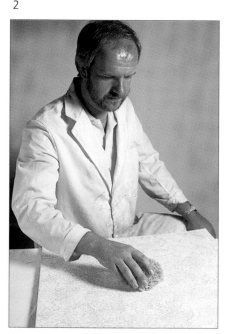

3

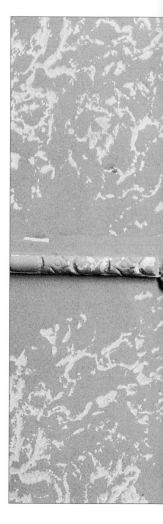

LEFT *Sponge on one colour or a whole sequence, letting each one dry before applying the next, depending on the complexity of colour-texture you want.*
1 The first, soft, semi-translucent green is sponged on airily.
2 Next, a slightly thicker gingery-beige, and rather more densely applied.
3 The third coat is a light, random sponging of butter yellow.

no pressure from the drying time of the glaze. Try experimenting with a patch first and if it is not a success, you can quickly wipe it off an oil-based ground with a rag and mineral spirits although, as with the other techniques, it is better to use pre-painted lining paper pinned to a board for testing.

There are an inspiring number of possible effects that can be achieved with sponging, since you have three variables – the glaze, which can be opaque, translucent, shiny or matt; the texture of the sponge (and the way you use it); plus the colours you choose. Sponging can be done with one or more colours. The freshest combinations come from pastels or clear, bright colours like emerald or tangerine used over white, but using a variety of tones

BELOW *The final touch proved to be a scattering of watery terracotta and sponging the radiator to match.*

LEFT *A complete face-lift for a pair of ordinary flush doors. First mouldings were stuck on to create panels and then a ground of very dusty pink applied as a foil for a sparse sponging of jade green.*

cloudier and the print less defined than with an oil-based paint, which gives a crisper, cleaner texture. For a translucent, marbled finish, use a tinted oil glaze. The best sponge to use is the genuine marine variety. But you can use a cellular sponge (massage sponges have an unusual texture); with the ordinary cellular type, cut it in half to get a flat surface and keep twisting it, with a flick of the wrist between dabs to disguise the regularity and hard edges of the print. It is also possible to 'sponge' with bunched-up rag; try out different weaves from muslin to burlap to find a texture you like, but whatever is used must be undyed and lint-free.

As well as paint/glaze and sponge/rags you will need a flat container to hold the sponging medium. An ordinary paint-tray (the kind used for roller-painting) is ideal as it will hold a reservoir of paint or glaze at the 'deep end', which can be tipped every now and then to leave a fresh film over the surface of the shallow end, where it can be picked up on the sponge. Clean paper and rags are essential.

in the same colour family, such as coffee over beige with perhaps a paler caramel sponged on top, produces a rich, mottled surface, often with the texture of rough stone. If the right colours are chosen, sponging can also look almost uncharacteristically smart and sophisticated. Imagine black sponged over a flannel grey, over electric blue or over scarlet. At the other extreme, you might want to create a soft cloud or colour with a combination like mauve and forest green sponged over sage. Whatever mixture you choose, sponging in two colours works best with the lighter colour on top.

■ *Materials and tools* This is one technique where it is both possible and easy to use latex but the effect will be

■ *Method* If you are using a marine sponge, soften it with mineral spirits first, or water if you are using emulsion, and let it expand to its full size, then wring it out thoroughly before using. Dab the sponge lightly on to the film of paint in the tray and test the print on clean paper before applying it to the wall. It will produce a wet, muddy print if there's too much paint on the sponge, so either squeeze it out or keep dabbing it on the paper until you get a soft but well-defined impression. Then start working your way over the wall with the sponge, refilling it as necessary and testing on spare paper each time, too, until you are confident of getting a consistent density of print without testing. If you are sponging with one colour only, overlap the prints slightly for an even, all-over texture; if you are planning to use more than one colour, keep the first sponge-prints fairly well

spaced out, wait for these to dry and
then fill in and partly overlap with prints
in the second colour. It is preferable to
try and avoid the kind of regularity of
pattern repeat found in bought
wallpaper or fabric, so make sure you
keep changing the position of the
sponge in your hand or, if you are using
rag, keep refolding and rebunching it.
Clean both every now and then, to save
getting messy prints, by rinsing out in
mineral spirits (water for latex) but
wringing both out thoroughly, otherwise
you'll dilute both glaze and print.

You can also sponge new colour on to
a *wet* ground, which will produce an
even softer print. In this case, follow the
procedure for stippling, ideally working
with two people, one applying the wet
ground colour in bands while the other
follows after, sponging on the second
colour.

RAG-ROLLING

Rag-rolling is one of the most dramatic
of the broken colour effects. It's related
to stippling, dragging and, of course,
ragging in that the relief patterning –
which can look unnervingly like crushed
silk or velvet – comes from partially
lifting the wet glaze off the ground, but
in this instance it's done by rolling a
sausage of bunched-up rag over the wet
glaze. The resulting pattern depends
very much on the type of rag used.
Cheesecloth, old sheeting or net curtain,
lace, linen, jute and burlap are all
possibilities as long as they are clean,
undyed and lint-free. The pattern they
produce varies with the softness of the
fabric from a distinct but subtle marl to
a crisp, definite marking, but all have a
certain formality.

There is no technical reason why you
shouldn't rag woodwork, but because its
application involves a considerable
amount of movement it is certainly
easier – and generally more appropriate
– to confine it to wide open spaces of
wall and ceiling. It is particularly good
at 'domesticating' these surfaces,

softening angles, visually amalgamating
oddly proportioned alcoves and
extrusions and giving depth, interest
and sophistication to otherwise boring
expanses of plasterwork.

Rag-rolling has such definite
markings that quite striking effects can
be achieved with the gentlest of colours,
so decorators tend to stick to the lighter
neutrals and more off-beat pastels over
a white or toning ground. A slightly dirty
white, tinted with a touch of raw umber
and raw sienna, which browns and 'ages'
it, makes a very sympathetic background
for deep, faded pastels like caramelled
pinks, dusty blues, greyish greens and
that unusual half-grey, half-buff colour
that some people call 'greige'. Even
rolling one shade of white over another
can produce interesting results: a speck
or two of black in a white glaze can
produce something like the light-and-
shade surface of an old damask
tablecloth. So experiment by all means
with bolder combinations, but softer
shades are a safer bet.

❚ *Equipment* Apart from paint for the
ground coat and mixed and tinted glaze

ABOVE *It's easy to tell
rag-rolling from
ragging because the
rolling technique
produces a much more
definite marl and a
distinct feeling of
movement.*

for the top, ragged coat, the usual paintbrushes are required, including a wide, soft one for applying the glaze, and above all a plentiful supply of your chosen rag. But only use one *type* of rag for each job, otherwise you will get differing textures.

■ *Method* With this technique you can afford to apply the glaze over a fairly large expanse of wall before beginning work on it with the rags, as rag-rolling is quite a quick process. (The exception, of course, is when latex paint is used. This dries so quickly that it is better to both paint and work on a sequence of narrow bands as well as having two people on the job, one painting and one rolling.) Make sure the glaze is well brushed out to a fine film, preferably with no brush marks. To lose all the brush marks, apply smaller areas of glaze at a time and rough-stipple them before you begin ragging. Roll the bunched-up sausage of rag across the glaze as if you were rolling pastry and, because, in this instance, you want an irregular effect, keep not only changing

direction, but rebunching the rag so that you don't produce too uniform a pattern. Each rag will have to be abandoned as the glaze begins to harden it, but chamois leather can be washed out in either mineral spirits or water, depending on the glaze, wringing it out thoroughly before you start ragging again. Some people prefer working with rag or chamois moistened in solvent (or water) as it produces a softer marl. Keep watching your work as it progresses and dab the rag directly on to the surface to fill in any missed or unsatisfactory areas, and near adjoining walls, ceiling or woodwork to save smudging them – the difference really will not show. You can also, of course, roll on a second colour once the first is dry, although sponging it on can look very pretty as it softens the ragged texture. As a general principle, a second glaze colour nearly always looks best if it is lighter than the first.

■ *Cleaning up* The danger of the solvent-and-glaze-saturated rags catching fire spontaneously if you leave

them bunched up in a confined space cannot be stressed too strongly. Make sure used rags are left out to dry before disposing of them.

STIPPLING

The traditional tool for stippling is a large, flat-faced soft-bristled stippling brush which, dabbed on to a wet glaze, lifts just enough of it for the background colour to show through, producing the fine, mottled, orange-peel texture typical of this finish. These brushes are extremely expensive, so you may well want to find an alternative. Experiment with a painters' dusting brush, a shoe brush, a soft-bristled hair brush, a worn down (or sawn off) broomhead; you could even try using a rubber-tipped stippling brush, usually used for textured paint, which is less expensive to buy but gives a much coarser finish. Each of these tools will produce a different texture, so it is worth testing them all to discover your preference but, whatever kind of brush you choose must have a flat bristle surface.

■ *Alternative tools to brushes* Brush-stippling can be quite a slow and exhausting business – although the bigger the brush, the quicker the ground can be covered, which makes the broomhead a popular choice, but there are several alternatives to brushes. You can stipple with clean, undyed, bunched-up rags, experimenting with different textures of fabric, or with sponges: the marine variety will produce a softer mottle, and for a crisp, granular stipple, cut a cellulose sponge in half to get a flat surface and keep twisting it from side to side as you stipple, to avoid too regular and hard-edged a pattern. Stippling can also be done with a roller – much the fastest way, although it's less easy to control the texture. Use lambswool, mohair (real or synthetic) or *coarse* polystyrene rollers (the smooth kind will just move the glaze about over the surface in nasty swirls) – each of these will give you a different finish, but they all leave a more blotchy, open texture than brush-stippling.

■ *Colours* The classic colour formula for stippling is to use a transparent or semi-transparent glaze over a white or at least light-coloured ground. The clean, solid colour of the glaze is lightened, softened and mottled by the tiny specks of ground showing through so that, for example, salmon pink over white or off-white becomes a velvety, pinky peach with a bloom that resembles the fruit itself; coffee on cream can look like natural suede. Only use this dark-on-light recipe as a guide rather than a limitation and experiment with your own colour combinations. Also, try matt over shiny finishes as well as mid-sheen over matt. Multi-colour finishes are also possible since stippling enables you to blend, say, two or three pastel shades into each other so that there's no clear demarcation line between the colours and the result is a cloud of shifting colour. You can stipple both walls and woodwork, but often it is better to keep one or other – that is, either walls or woodwork – plain, rather than treating both, to make a satisfying crispness of contrast.

■ *Equipment* Apart from your chosen stippling tool (brush, rag, sponge or roller), ground colour, glaze and the material for thinning and tinting, you will need a couple of paintbrushes – use a wide, flat brush for applying the glaze – and plenty of clean rags or paper for wiping tools and mopping up.

LEFT *Even though brush-stippling from a distance, probably comes closest to a plain surface, there is still a misty quality to the colour and closer inspection reveals a very definite texture.*

■ *Method* It really couldn't be simpler. Once the ground colour is on and dry and the glaze mixed, you just brush on a band of glaze – about 2 ft (60 cm) wide is the most workable width – and then stipple over it. There are just one or two points to watch for, depending on which stippling tool is being used. If you choose a brush, rag or sponge it is much more helpful to have two people on the job, one to paint and the other to follow on stippling, so that there is no panic about keeping a wet edge going. The glaze should be brushed out thoroughly to a fine, even film and the stippling done by pressing the tool flat to the surface with a smooth but decisive dabbing motion, above all avoiding skids. Do not change roles halfway, as one stippler's touch is always different from another's and this difference will show.

Whatever the stippling tool, you will reach a point where it is so loaded with glaze that you risk putting more on than you're taking off. Clean brushes regularly by wiping them on clean paper or rags; change stippling rags frequently or clean the rags and sponge by rinsing them out in mineral spirits. Some people actually prefer to work with sponge or rags moistened with solvent as it tends to 'open out' the texture on the glaze. Keep a watch on your work too: any missed patches can be filled by brushing a thin film of glaze across the bristle-tips of the stippling brush or the face of the rag or sponge and dabbing it on the bare patch. This is a safer rescue method than brushing on more glaze, as long as you clean any excess glaze off the brush, rag/sponge before moving on. A clean stippling tool should also reduce any over-glazed or twice-glazed areas of darker colour, although it may need to be moistened with mineral spirits for obstinate areas where the glaze has started to harden.

Roller stippling is so quick that it can easily be managed by just one person – it is actually quicker to stipple the glaze off than it is to paint it on. The only points to watch for are keeping the pressure even so that the texture remains regular and to avoid skidding – otherwise you will take too much colour off and will have to re-cover the patch with glaze, then stipple over it again. As with the other tools, keep the roller clean by rolling it out regularly on clean paper to remove surplus glaze.

■ *Cleaning up* Clean rollers on paper, as above, before squeezing them out in mineral spirits. Clean sponges and brushes with mineral spirits, too. If you throw the rags away, make sure you spread them out to dry first; when soaked with a mixture of paint/glaze and solvent, they are highly inflammable and could combust spontaneously if they are left bunched up in a waste basket.

Spattering has a very different feeling from the other effects, partly because it is generally a more casual and informal finish (although this also depends, of course, on the colours chosen) and partly because the 'spattering' of specks and flecks of paint on to walls or woodwork actually creates more of a texture, and a surface that is almost three-dimensional. It tends to be a

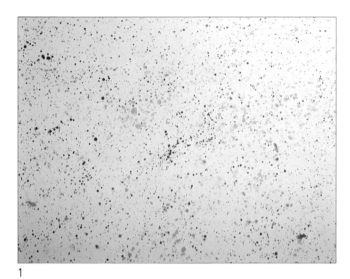

1

2

3

Spattering can be done in one or more colours but it generally looks best if the whole effect remains fairly open.
1 The first, sparse spattering of red is showered on to a white ground.
2 Yellow and mid-green have been used equally sparingly and now a faint freckling of a watery dark green is being applied.
3 This darker green gives a bit of 'bite' to the final colouring, balancing the red and saving the whole from being too wishy-washy.

messy process, so cover up anything that you don't want freckled with paint – including yourself – so that you can work freely.

■ *Colours* If you use close tones of the same colour or different colours of the same tonal value, a mist effect is created, which is much more suited to – and better achieved with – one of the other techniques such as sponging or stippling. Try spattering for nursery-like gaiety and freshness, using primary colours or the gayer and brighter of the pastels flicked on to white; for startling combinations like yellow, pink and black flicked on to grey. Use spattering for sophistication, too, and for its ability to intensify or subdue an existing colour: a brilliant cornflower over a calm saxe blue creates more surface 'tension' and excitement than either colour could provide on its own, whereas spattering glossy black over a rich, mid-sheen bottle green changes the latter's rather claustrophobic sombreness to the iridescent sheen of a bluebottle. The contrast of paint finishes is another important and useful element in spattering, because, luckily, any paint that can be diluted to a liquid, flickable state can be used. Run through colour combinations in your mind and imagine how they would look if either ground or spatter were shiny, low-lustre or matt.

■ *Equipment* A stencil brush is the ideal tool because of its stiff, squared off bristles, but an ordinary, rather coarse-bristled paintbrush will do if the bristles are sliced off squarely to about half their length. You will also need the relevant solvents and tinting agents for thinning and mixing paint, clean cans to mix it in, plus paper to experiment, pre-painted the colour of your ground.

■ *Method* With spattering it really is a good idea to spend time experimenting first. You will want to test not only your own spattering touch, but paint consistency too. For a good spray the paint should not be thicker than a milk-like consistency, but if it is made too thin it will run down instead of holding to the wall. Practise diluting a small amount of paint at a time, noting what proportion of solvent you need to add to get the right mix. To 'spatter', dip the bristle-tips of the brush into the paint then slide your finger, a knife or a comb steadily across the bristles to release a fine spray. With practice, you will be able to vary the size of the droplets in the spray and aim them with surprising accuracy. When spattering in more than one colour, leave the first coat to dry before starting the next and protect the final result with varnish, which is especially important where water-based paints are used.

DRAGGING AND COMBING

These effects are decorative extensions of graining, with the main difference that the aim here is not to simulate 'the real thing' or even a stylized version of it. Nevertheless, both these techniques – and the distinction between them is made mainly by the equipment used – can definitely produce effects that resemble materials other than paint. One-way dragging of a wet glaze with a dry brush, normally used vertically, produces fine, slightly irregularly spaced lines as the brush reveals some of the ground colour and leaves a surface texture like woven cotton with a heavily slubbed weft. But a second glaze colour can be applied and dragged either vertically or horizontally, in the latter case producing a texture like raw silk. And both the vertical and horizontal dragging can be in bands, so that something like a plaid effect is achieved.

Combing – either with proper steel or rubber graining combs or homemade versions cut from rubber or plastic flooring – obviously results in coarser lines than the the dragging brush and a mixture of the two can produce some very exciting effects. The choice of both

BELOW *By dragging with the flat-faced brush made for the job it is rather easier to obtain fine, clean, straight lines. However, unless you are really doing a lot of dragged work, the difference in the result is not enough to compensate for the difference in brush prices. Here, you can see the effects produced by a dusting brush (a paper-hanging brush would do just as well) and by dragging twice with the dry brush.*

LEFT *Even close-up, dragging retains its resemblance to open-weave textile, although variations from the true vertical give it away. But these really don't matter, you're not trying actually to fake fabric and these imperfections, if not too frequent or at too marked an angle, can serve to make the surface more interesting.*

colours and paint finishes enormously changes the character of a dragged or combed finish. One-way dragging of tone on tone with flat-oil paint or undercoat in, say, brick over terracotta can be subtle, formal and smart – a suitable setting for the elegant polished wood tables and chairs of a town house dining room. But it can also look pale and bedroom-pretty in pastels on white and works equally well in more adventurous combinations such as charcoal over scarlet. At the other extreme, combing a shiny glaze in different directions all over a low-lustre finish, so that the light is bounced off the surface at all angles, produces a surface ripple like shot silk.

Both dragging and combing can be used on plaster and wood surfaces, even on floors. However, for one-way dragging, in particular, it is important that the wall surface is sound, smooth and even as, unlike some of the other finishes, the lines created by dragging serve only to emphasize irregularities.

▌ *Tools and materials* Like many of the specialist brushes, those made for dragging are considerably more expensive than ordinary paintbrushes so

it is only worth buying one if it will really earn its cost. Alternatives are a wide paper-hanging brush or a jamb duster. Graining combs are less expensive, but you can still make or buy alternatives. Make them by cutting V-shaped notches in plastic or rubber flooring, either at regular or irregular intervals. Buy large, wide-toothed plastic hair combs or metal combs, which can be adapted to produce an irregular pattern by bending back or breaking off some of the teeth.

Although it is possible to drag an oil glaze over an emulsion ground – a quick

LEFT *Here, the glaze has been sparingly and brushily, but evenly laid over the ground and the dragged result is light and open.*

BELOW *This extraordinary, variegated plaid effect is produced by combing the glaze horizontally first, overlaid with wavy lines, and then vertically in straight lines.*

1

2

3

Combing sequence
1 A soft brush lays on a loose paint gloss.
2 A coarse rubber comb straightens the lines.
3 A stiff, fine comb gives a kinked, herringbone texture.
4 The same technique applied again, at right

angles, creates a woven effect.
5 A fine rubber comb can be used to create a semicircular fish-scale pattern, often seen on plaster.
6 A broad fish-scale pattern is achieved with a soft rubber comb.

4

and unusual way of reviving a tired colour scheme – dragging is most successful over a ground of either flat oil paint, undercoat or eggshell. This is not only because their non-absorbent surfaces make it easier to manipulate the glaze, but because, particularly with combing, their harder skins are more resilient to the pressure of rubber or steel. For the most clearly defined, dragged coat, with a shiny, washable finish, use a translucent oil glaze. The next best thing to this is a mixture of glaze and oil-based paint, which has more opacity. Some decorators do simply thin eggshell to near-

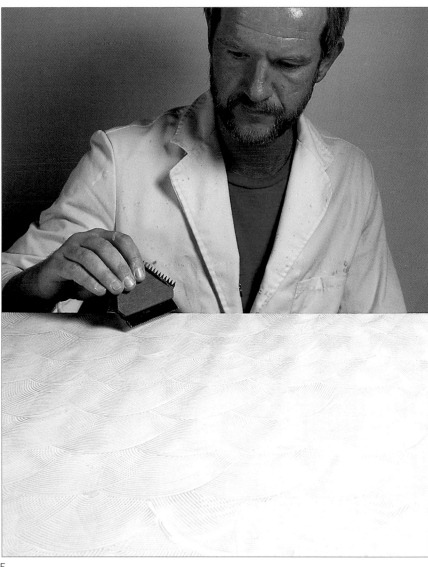

5

6

transparency with mineral spirits, but the quicker drying of this mixture makes it harder to keep a wet edge going. For a flatter finish, use flat oil paint or undercoat; the stripes tend to merge together more, but you may like this effect. Dragging with thinned emulsion gives the flattest finish of all, but it has its own charm and may appeal. Whenever you thin or tint paint or glaze, experiment on paper or board with both tools and materials to be sure of colour, paint/glaze consistency and the effect of brush and comb before starting. Keep clean paper, rags and mineral spirits handy for wiping tools and mopping up.

WALLS

Dragging or combing a wall becomes a smoother operation with two people, one to apply the vertical bands of colour, about 2 ft (60 cm) wide, the other to drag it straight and steady from top to bottom. With this technique, it is especially important to keep the wet edge 'alive' and the directional nature of the effect will only emphasize the patchiness of any overlap of wet colour on dry. Keep the glaze well brushed out to a fine, even film to prevent it running and always make the last, laying-off stroke downwards to avoid a criss-cross

effect when the glaze is dragged. The hardest part in dragging is to keep the dragged lines straight and true. At the same time, being tense and apprehensive will only lessen your chances of success. Try to stay relaxed and relatively loose-wristed. Simply rest the bristle-tips on the surface and keep the pressure even as you drag the brush down the wall. If you doubt your ability to maintain a reasonably straight, vertical line, suspend a plumb from ceiling to floor an inch or so away from the wall, moving it along as you move yourself; or use the decorators' trick of a straight-edged board with nails knocked through to keep it off the wall (tie a spirit level to the board for level, horizontal dragging). If there is simply no way of doing top-to-bottom in one swoop, stop the down-stroke somewhere between waist-level and skirting board – that is below eye-level, standing or sitting – and brush upwards to meet it, feathering the join lightly and staggering the level of these joins so that you don't get a stripe of feathering across the wall.

When dragging, wipe the glaze off the dry brush between strokes or you will be putting colour on rather than taking it

off and the definition of the stripes will vary. Watch, too, for a build-up of glaze at top and bottom of the wall – lighten pressure here and around switches and mouldings and keep a mineral-spirits-soaked rag handy for smudges. If you are planning to add a second, dragged coat, let the first dry thoroughly before reglazing and give the final surface a coat of clear matt or semi-gloss varnish – optional for oil-based glazes, essential for water-based.

WOODWORK

Although the scale of the job will differ from walls, requiring small brushes, the method is basically the same. The important point to watch with woodwork is to follow the direction of the grain –

or the direction in which it would normally run, even if it cannot be seen. This is especially important on panelled doors and on windows, for even though you are not trying to simulate wood grain, it will simply look odd if the dragging is in one direction across all the broken surfaces. Follow the painting sequence and glaze/drag in one grain-direction at a time, masking off the other section and waiting until the first set of dragging is dry before working on the next. Emphasize the joins or joints between sections either with a fine, painted line (in a slightly deeper tone of the dragged colour or in a watery neutral-like grey or buff to suggest shadow), or you can make a light knife-score, which is then lined with the sharpened point of a lead pencil.

ABOVE *Dragging gives a clean, subtly aged quality, where broken colour might have become disjointed, and lends an air of elegant restraint to the potentially busy design of carpet and furniture.*

RIGHT *In this bedroom the walls have been dragged vertically to resemble loosely woven cloth. The picture rail and cornice have been dragged but the edge-beading left plain.*

FLOORS

Dragging can be rather too fine and subtle an effect for a floor, whereas combing can add pattern, colour sophistication and gaiety to both floorboards and chipboard or hardboard floors. Although, if they are laid close enough together, the directional nature of floorboards can be disguised with painted panels. Boards look good simply combed in one colour over the ground, in the direction of the grain. This still leaves you plenty of decorative scope, as colour possibilities can range from light and pretty, like mid-grey dragged over white, to something dark and dramatic like black over red. Hardboard and chipboard panels can take some very

jazzy treatments and it's astounding the range of designs, from simple, straight-line geometrics to complex curves, that a simple tool like a comb can produce. One way to think of such a project is as if you were creating your own, large- or small-scaled, 'tiled' floor, and, with this in mind, carry out the combing accordingly.

■ *Materials* Stick to flat-oil paint, undercoat or eggshell for floors. Prime new wood, then undercoat the floor and apply at least two coats of undiluted, or only very slightly thinned, paint to provide a good, solid ground. The combing coat should be thinned less for floors than for other surfaces (about a 1:3 mixture of mineral spirits to paint),

again to give adequate 'body' to the finish.

■ *Method* Whatever type of floor you're painting, don't forget to paint yourself out of, not into, the room! With floorboards, start in the opposite corner from the doorway and follow the principles for one-way dragging, painting and combing a couple of boards at a time. The advantage of laying a new hardboard/chipboard floor, is being able to paint and comb the panels before you lay them. If the panels are already down, the easiest way to keep the edges neat is to do them a chequerboard sequence (as if you were working first on all the white squares on a chessboard, then on the black), masking the edges each time

and waiting until the first set is dry before masking, painting and combing the second. Either way, plan the floor out on paper first, so you know exactly what you're doing, and use chalk lines to snap the position of panel edges on to the floor if they won't correspond exactly with the panels as laid: it may be, for example, that the chipboard is laid in rectangles where square panels are wanted. Once the combing coat is dry, protect the finish with polyurethane varnish – two coats will give you a certain degree of protection, but three coats will give real durability against the inevitable wear and tear that any floor will receive. It is always worth taking the trouble to apply these extra coats.

FANTASY DECORATION

Such are the miraculous properties of paint that it can be used, and has been by generations of decorators and craftsmen, to simulate natural materials, from everyday substances such as wood and bamboo to exquisites like fine marble and tortoiseshell. Paint can also be used to simulate age – the patina of decades, even centuries of wear, newly created. It is these types of finishes that are covered by this section, together with two basic suggestions to anyone attempting them. The first is that, as a general principle, you confine your use of these finishes to surfaces that might just conceivably be made of their originals. This is not a hard-and-fast rule and the second point can explain why. Although some of the decision-making about how and where to use what is down to aesthetic instinct, the innate behaviour and traditional use of the original material – such as whether it normally has a flat or curved face, whether or not it can be carved – act as a useful guide. The second suggestion, then, is don't aim for perfection. It takes not only talent but years of practice to reproduce the appearance of these natural materials so exactly that they might be mistaken for the real thing. The amateur decorator is unlikely to be able to achieve this degree of verisimilitude and anyway, it is unnecessary and probably not what is wanted.

The essence, or fantasy, of these finishes is their impressionistic quality: in using the appropriate patterning and colour, they offer a general impression of the original material, but the purpose is decorative effect, not a mirror up to nature. This allows for a certain amount of license, within reason, to use these 'fakes' on some surfaces where the original would have been either impossible or ridiculously extravagant – for example, in tortoiseshelling a wall. Practically, these techniques are within the reach of anyone who has the confidence and will take the care to try them.

Painted marble, porphyry and wood grain are among the oldest and most beautiful of decorators' crafts, transforming walls, ceilings and furniture alike. Painted tortoiseshell and bamboo offer an exotic panache to smaller items, from banisters and coffee tables to clocks, watch-cases and picture frames.

MARBLING

There are as many paint techniques for marbling as there are types of marble. No decorative technique relies so heavily on the natural behaviour of paint and its reaction to the materials used with it; no technique is so full of surprises and delights and, in some ways, there is no technique in which it is easier to produce such extraordinary results since, to a large extent and with the aid of a few simple tools and accessories, the materials do the work for you. However, it is essential to know what these materials are and how to use them. Results are assured by following certain guidelines.

It is also helpful to understand something of the basic structure of marble in order to attempt even a merely decorative facsimile. The most important thing to understand is that marble was originally created by movement: by the action of heat and pressure on limestone, which caused crystalization in black, white and other, sometimes brilliant, colours; by mineral substances running through the original molten strata and cooling in vein-like form; by the fragmenting of layers like leaves in a book, whose cracks became filled with other, variegated matter before the whole welded itself together as solid stone. But marble isn't, in fact, 'solid' – at least to the eye. Its translucent quality results in some veins and colourings showing clearly and strongly on the surface while others are seen more vaguely beneath it. Real marble has movement, a directional flow and a mixture of opacity and translucency; and so, of course, does paint.

Marbling has long been an inspiration and a challenge to painters, proven by examples dating back as early as 2000BC, and some exceptionally fine examples exist. In today's interiors, marbling works well on walls, skirting board, mantelpieces and floors – and best, with the possible exception of matching mantelpieces and skirting board, if its use is restricted to one of these areas per room. As with the other techniques in this section, the aim is not necessarily to reproduce the original exactly or even attempt the accuracy of the grand marbling masters. Merely approximating some of the colours and forms can produce delightful and different effects, which have a decorative value in their own right and marbling can be anything you make it.

SICILIAN MARBLE

This is one of the simplest marbles to imitate; it is white with tinges of light greeny grey, yellow and soft, but with

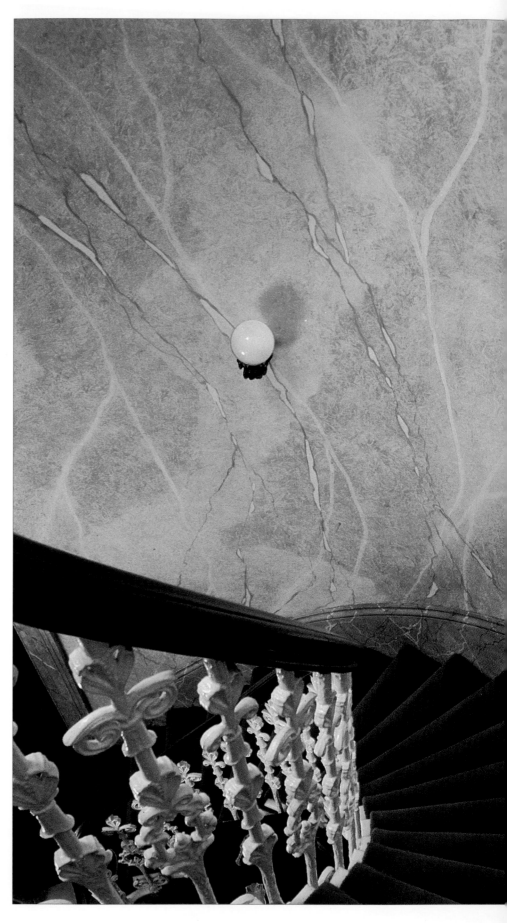

LEFT *This marbled stairwell attempts a fake finish. Because it's done in a stylized way (see closeup above), it comes off.*

RIGHT *The combination of marbling with other surface effects is unusual but often works well.*

distinctive veins in black and a dark, warm grey.

▮ *Materials* The ground should be in a dead white flat oil paint, eggshell or undercoat and well rubbed down with fine abrasive paper when dry to eliminate brush marks and leave a smooth flat surface. For marbling you will need transparent oil glaze; boiled linseed oil; artists' oil colour in Chinese white, black, raw umber and pale yellow ochre; two oil crayons, one in a warm grey and the other black; a small marine sponge; a softening brush (the specialist version, again quite expensive, is a hog-hair softener but a soft 2 or 3 in (5 or 7.5cm) paintbrush will do); saucers, screw-top jars, clean rags and mineral spirits.

▮ *Method I* Prepare all the materials in advance. Blend a little of the white oil or colour with the oil to make a milky, near-transparent mixture. Prepare small amounts each of two pale shades of glaze – a grey-green (white plus raw umber plus a little black) and a yellowish grey (white plus raw umber plus a little yellow plus a little black) – by dissolving the oil colour in mineral spirits and adding an equal amount of glaze. Now, use a rag to rub the surface all over with the white oil mixture. Then use first the grey crayon to draw in the inner veins, followed by the black crayon to add the more prominent outer ones. The veins should meander across the surface diagonally, branching to left and right from a central point and then linking up again to make quite large-scale, rough and irregular diamond shapes. Veining lines are never straight but vary, rather like an erratic old sewing machine, from patches of quite frantic zig-zagging to calm ripples across

1

2

3

4

5

6

1 An ochre glaze is laid brushily over the creamy-white ground, so that a lot of the background still shows through, and then supplemented by diagonal loops and swirls of dark brown.
2 Colours are blended and brush-marks partly obliterated by dabbing the surface, while still wet, with crumpled newspaper.
3 The whole effect is softened with a dry brush, drawn diagonally across the surface first one way and then the other.
4 Veins are fidgeted in with a slim artists' brush in sepia and blue glaze so near transparent that some colour is taken off the surface as these are added.
5 The new veins are teased with a feather to soften their lines.
6 As a final touch, the whole surface is softened and blended again with light, diagonal sweeps of a soft-bristled, dry brush.

the surface. The end result should look very much like the wanderings of rivers, streams and tributaries across a map, with one exception: the veins always have a beginning and an end, they do not just appear from nowhere, nor do they disappear into nothing. Keep the veins well spaced-out, with just occasional busy patches where one set crosses another, but err on the side of too few veins rather than too many. Fill in the patches between them by sponging in areas of the grey-green and yellowish grey glaze but, again, be sparing and don't entirely cover the white ground. The last step is, with the dry paintbrush, to stroke the whole surface diagonally, first in one direction, then the other. This is where the transformation occurs and as the crayon lines soften and glazes the blend, the whole thing suddenly does begin to look like a piece of marble.

■ *Method II* Another method, which produces a very similar effect, involves covering the ground with a thin, pale, greeny grey paint glaze. A 1:2 mixture of paint and mineral spirits, plus a little raw umber and black, it should have just enough colour to show against the white ground when it is sponged on. Veins can then be added – in two different mixtures of raw umber and black to give a lighter and darker shade – with a fine, pointed artists' brush. The brush is teased against the direction of the vein to produce the more excited, zig-zag lines; for the smoother, rippling lines, hold the brush straight out, like an extension of your hand and, with palm upwards, rotate the brush as you draw it towards you across the surface, varying the pressure to vary the line width. These lines can be sponged lightly and a little of the dark colour transferred from the sponge to the areas between them before softening the surface with diagonal brush strokes.

Veins can also be drawn in with a feather, either by using the tip as the finest of paintbrushes or by irregularly

serrating the broad edge. Dip this edge first in water, then in mineral spirits, comb it to separate the fronds, brush some oil colour on to it and draw it across the surface. It will leave a set of fine lines which, when the feather is turned sharply, will branch off in all directions; and by simply changing your hand to the other diagonal, the movement will be along rather than across the feather, the lines will all join sharply at different points to become a single vein.

SERPENTINE MARBLE

This is one of the most dramatic marbles which, for painting purposes at least, has a black ground, mottled with slightly dusty emerald and streaked with a random criss-crossing of straightish, thread-like white veins. This is almost simpler to simulate than Sicilian, except that this technique needs to be executed on a horizontal surface or the paint and solvent will run. Lay the ground as before with black oil-based paint. Mix a top coat of green paint glaze – emerald with just a touch each of raw umber and black to 'dirty' it, thinning no more than one part mineral spirits to two parts paint, so the glaze has a reasonable amount of body. Apply the glaze and then flick random splashes of mineral spirits over it with a stiff stencil brush. Wherever these splashes fall they will magically open up the glaze to reveal the ground. This phenomenon is technically known as 'cissing' and the shapes produced can be varied by flicking on methylated spirits or plain water (keep cotton buds handy to neatly soak up any over-enthusiastic splashes). Now, squeezing a marine sponge out in thin white paint glaze, dab it here and there on the revealed areas of ground so that there is the occasional light mottling of white. Lastly, coat lengths of cotton twine with white oil colour laying them on the surface to produce a loose, random lattice-work of fine, diagonal veins.

ROSE MARBLE

■ Application

Method I This marble can have a base colour of soft, sandy gold – beige with yellow added and a spot of red – with a pale pink glaze brushed over it. This glaze can be applied so that there are corridors or canals where the base colour is left to show through. These unglazed, linear patches may be quite wide – up to 6in (15cm) – so that they form wide, sandy veins across the rose-coloured areas. Then, mix a glaze of 4:1 parts blue to red, with a touch of white and a trace of burnt umber to give a grey-purple. Sponge or brush this loosely over the pink-glazed areas. After this, dab the surface with a crumpled newspaper to give a soft, creasing effect. Veins of thin white can then be traced on to the surface with a feather or an artists' brush, crossing over the purple/

pink areas as well. The whole surface is finally softened again with a dry brush. *Method II* A matt coat of deep pink or grey-pink – magenta, white and a touch of black or grey – should be laid on over a light grey base coat, in the same way that the white ground is laid over the base coat in Sicilian marble. This should be over-glazed with a thin white paint glaze, followed by an ochre glaze laid in rough, feathery diagonals. These should be softened with a dry brush dispensing with any hard lines which might spoil the overall effect and then, either with a feather or artists' brush, a deeper blue and red glaze should be applied to evoke veins, roughly following the ragged, softened ochre veins. To finish off, as with the first method; the whole surface may be softened with a dry brush for a more naturalistic appearance.

BLACK SERPENTINE MARBLE

The first method given for simulating serpentine marble is simpler to execute than the Sicilian effect, except that it needs to be done horizontally because of the flow of the paint. The second is perhaps rather less easy, but allows a vertical approach. In either case, black serpentine is a very beautiful and dramatic marble and should be simulated sparingly. In small amounts it can be superb, *en masse* it tends to be somewhat oppressive.

■ Application

Method I For purposes of simulation, at least, serpentine has a black ground, mottled with a dusty emerald and streaked with random, thread-like veins of white. Lay the ground with black, oil-based paint, then mix the top coat of green paint glaze – emerald with a touch

1

2

3

4

5

LEFT AND ABOVE *The starting point for this marbled pillar was a plain, creamy-white ground. The steps for achieving a similar effect are shown above.*

ABOVE *White marbling sequence. 1 Black thinned to a grey glaze is dabbed on with a creased newspaper. 2 The surface is then softened with a dry brush. 3 Grey veins are applied using an artists brush. 4 These are softened and smudged again with a cloth. 5 The whole effect is crossed again with a dry brush, to produce a delicate misty result.*

ABOVE *Rose marble and pink-veined white: two effects achieved by reversing the same colours, rather like a photographic negative. Note the broad fluidity of the veins on the right and the delicacy of those on the left.*

you to achieve this effect on a vertical surface. A black, oil-based ground should be applied in the usual manner, and over this a black oil-based coat, thinned in a ratio of 1:2 parts mineral spirits to paint. This should be laid on so that there are still patches exposing the dry base coat and also thin linear areas of veins joined to these patches. While this is still wet, unthinned latex in white or very light grey can be taken up very thickly with a marine sponge and dabbed lightly on the surface where the wet, black glaze coat has not been applied. You will find that latex will flow into the wet edge of the oil. Using either a feather or a thin artists' brush, held in the manner described for Sicilian marble, roll the latex along the linear vein spaces left in the oil coat, fairly liberally, teasing it into the edges of the oil coat. You will have islands of hazy swirling mottle where the sponge has been, linked by hazy veins of white. Add very fine lines by laying cotton strands, liberally coated with latex, against the wet oil surface; hold them at both ends and slap them against the surface. The natural action of the water-based paint floating on the oil surface often means the surface doesn't need brushing afterwards, but a dry brush can be used to soften areas where the effect is in any way short of the desired finish. Over this, when dry, should go a thin, emerald glaze. When this has dried, the surface should be given a clear coat of matt or semi-gloss varnish to prevent a different texture occurring and catching the light between the two types of paint. Brushes used for this process should be washed out in mineral spirits and then warm, soapy water.

of raw umber and black to dirty it or take the edge off it. Mix this in a ratio of 1:2 parts mineral spirits to paint, so that the glaze has a reasonable body. When you've applied the glaze, take a stiff brush and splash mineral spirits at random all over it by flicking the brush. Where the mineral spirits fall, irregular apertures will open in the glaze to reveal the black ground, a process known as cissing, an effect that can also be obtained by flicking water over oil-based paint. Next, squeeze a marine sponge out in thin white paint glaze and dab it on the areas of black ground revealed by the cissing, so that an occasional mottle of white results. For the veins, it is highly effective to coat lengths of cotton thread or thicker twine in white oil colour and lay them on the surface to produce a random flow and an occasionally crossing fretwork of fine, diagonal lines.

Method II This involves using oil- and water-based paint together, and enables

RED MARBLE

Rose marble has a soft, glowing quality to it, whereas red marble has a deep, sumptuous appearance, the difference perhaps between silk and velvet. Like black serpentine, the red marble pattern is exotic and best used sparingly. Its ground is an orangey magenta, rather like a punch made of red wine and pineapple juice. The grain or vein of this marble evokes a ragged white net or the diamond-shaped mesh of a wire fence that is encrusted with ice and torn in places.

▋ *Application*

Method I Over a dark grey or brick-red base coat, brush or sponge a ground colour of 4:1 parts deep pink to yellow ochre with a touch of blue thinned by about a third with mineral spirits. Mix an off-white glaze – flake white and yellow ochre – and, using a feather, simulate a wide-spaced version of the mesh pattern. Soften this pattern by crossing the edges of it lightly with a dry brush, leaving the central strokes of the veins fairly crisp. When this has dried, go over the whole with a thin, light blue glaze. Finally, in the centre of the junctions where the veins of the grid cross, use an artists' brush or half a potato to add flecks of deeper magenta or magenta and blue.

Method II This is a similar technique to that of using oil- and water-based paint to simulate black serpentine. After applying a brick-red base coat, apply a second of the same colour with a trace of blue and a touch of yellow ochre. While this is still wet, float an off-white, ragged mesh pattern of latex over it in the manner used for black serpentine. When this has dried, the veins may be strengthened with a feather.

Method III This is an exact reversal of the preceding technique. Over the base coat of brick-red, apply the ragged vein mesh with off-white, oil-based paint, using an artists' brush or large feather. Then fill in the areas between the veins with latex. Where you brush or sponge the latex up against the oil-based veins, a soft swirling and bending will occur, and fine wisps of the oil-based paint will be carried like threads into the latex. This is perhaps easier to apply than Method II, as oil-based paint is more dominating than water-based, and in the second method there can be a danger of

the water-based veins being 'drowned' in the oil surface and disintegrating. This third method is also rather quicker, as the quick-drying latex means that at least two-thirds of the area is dry and can easily be touched up while the remainder is blending, while in Method II, the whole surface is liable to be wet for a considerable time before you can strengthen any areas that are not satisfactory.

GREEN OR TERRA VERDE MARBLE

This is probably one of the most attractive of marble patterns, as it has the panache of black serpentine but is less stark. Its salient features are a moss-green ground with shifting, deep blue clouds across it, veins of ochre and gold and then serpentine veins of white crossing the deep blue-green. Occasionally it may have a gold flecking, achieved by a very fine spattering.

ABOVE *A green marbled, varnished mantelpiece joins a ragged amber glaze chimney-piece and a yellow Sicilian marble.*

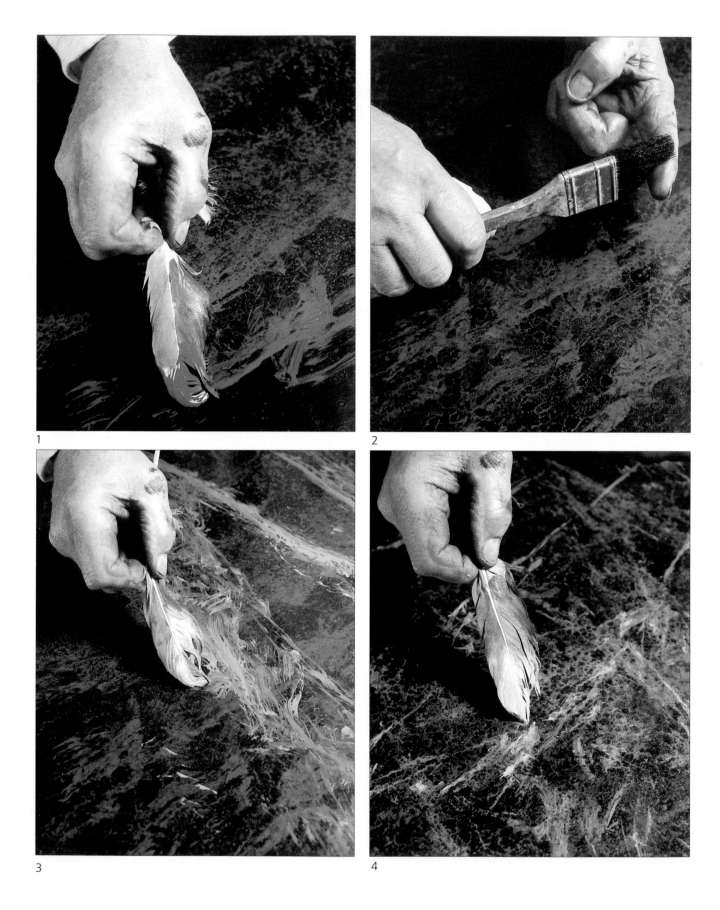

1

2

3

4

■ *Application* Over a base colour of flat-oil, undercoat or eggshell in a dark- or mid-green, apply a paint glaze of 3:1 parts artists' oil paint to mineral spirits, to give a blue-green clouded effect. This oil colour should be 3 parts ultramarine blue, 1 part emerald and 1 part burnt umber. Brush or sponge this glaze liberally all over the base colour, leaving sizeable areas uncovered by it. Then, using an artists' brush or a feather, add the yellow veins: they should consist of an oil glaze with 3 parts yellow ochre, 1 part red and 1 part white, and be allowed to meander as they do in Sicilian marble. Cross the veins with a dry brush to soften their lines and, if necessary, strengthen the inner parts of the veins afterwards. Then, using lengths of cotton thread soaked in white oil paint, lay sinuous, white veins across the blue-green areas between the yellow veins. The yellow veins should be much broader and more powerful than these thin, white lines; all are diagonal, but the white should appear like little shoals of eels passing through wide, green spaces in a gold mesh net.

If you want to create the effect of gold flecking, take a dry 3in or 4in (7.5cm or 10cm) brush and coat the ends of the bristles with gold enamel paint. You may need to thin this paint slightly with mineral spirits, about 1:4 parts mineral spirits to paint but no more. Hold the brush 6–12in (15–30cm) from the surface and run a steel-toothed comb across the bristles in a single saw-stroke, to give a soft spray. The flecked areas occur in the blue-green patches among the thin, white veins. It is somewhat easier to use this method than a canned spray, which tends to give too dense a delivery to the surface of this marble.

BLUE MARBLE

This is an effect like deep blue, clouded glass. The base colour should be a flat-oil, undercoat or eggshell in mid-blue, and over this a series of glazes is applied, more evenly spread than for most marbles.

■ *Application* Mix a thin oil glaze of ultramarine, 1:2 parts paint to glaze, and brush it all over the base colour. Then, using a feather or artists' brush, lay swirling veins into this glaze, in an off-white paint glaze – 3:1 parts paint to mineral spirits. This resembles Sicilian marble but is more fluid, like cigarette smoke. Over these and the blue areas, apply another thin, blue glaze so that the whole effect is pale and deep blue. Next should go a slightly thicker coloured glaze of magenta, leaving some patches uncovered to give a purple-blue, bruising effect; then, using cotton lines coated with white paint, add thin white lines along these bruised areas. Soften the whole with a dry brush, giving a thin, overall glaze of emerald as a finishing touch.

OTHER TECHNIQUES

The preceding marbles are an example and guide. To begin to enumerate all the possible colours and variations of this stone would be to recite the colour wheel in the form of veins and grounds and base coats. There is simply no limit to the colours you can choose and the only limits to the technique are set by the materials you use. With an oil-based paint glaze, mixed 1:1 with mineral spirits, you can virtually marble on any ground in any colour. You can mix three or four glazes of different colours and spread them over the ground and blend them, dabbing the whole surface with a marine sponge or creased paper. By adding transparent oil glazes of lighter and darker hues, you can create a feeling of depth in the finish that is peculiar to marble as a polished rock and gives it that element of clouds and tinted veils that is the prime secret of its light-retaining quality. Spattering any colour in showers of fine flecks can be effective, provided that it isn't overdone, as most marbles do not include too many of these isolated crystals. However,

LEFT: *Sequence for green marble*
1 *Broad ruffles of green glaze are applied over black with a feather.*
2 *The surface is cissed with mineral spirits, sprayed from a bristle brush, to open up the pattern.*
3 *A mixed green and white paint glaze is feathered cross-wise over the preceding green veins.*
4 *Fine white veins finish the effect.*

oil – a mixture of 1:6 parts boiled linseed oil to mineral spirits – should be brushed over it. On to that should be brushed a really thin solution of the ground colour, diluted with mineral spirits until positively watery. Using two or three other colours to the same level of dilution, and ¼–½in (6–12mm) brushes, dab these colours on the wet ground. They will flow together with ease – in fact, so easily that you may have to dab them with cotton batting squeezed out in mineral spirits. If, for some reason, they are reluctant to flow, dab more mineral spirits on with cotton batting. When they have dried sufficiently, veining over them can be achieved by any of the methods already mentioned, particularly with cotton twine lines, although this has to be executed flat.

■ *Paper rocking* One of the quickest, most effective methods of simulating marble, and very subtle and gentle in appearance, is moving newspaper or another thin, easily crinkled paper over the surface glaze. A thin paint glaze of just off-white or a very delicate blue-grey or pale ochre gold can be evenly spread over a base of matt white; the paper, which must be creased or pleated beforehand, is then laid against this. Where the creases come against the glaze they will raise or absorb it, leaving fine, vein-like lines. If the paper is then pushed or stroked with a stiff brush against the surface, it will shift the glaze surface, blending different colours together. This rocking of the paper will give a softer, more subtle transition and sense of movement than any other equally quick method. If the glaze is a soft monotone, such as pale grey-blue or ochre, the result will be highly realistic when the paper is removed. If the glaze is varicoloured, because the fine vein lines will cross different shaded areas without relating to them, the result will be less realistic but very pleasing, evoking the general visual atmosphere of marble rather than its actual appearance.

spattering mineral spirits or wood alcohol in the same way – even on a vertical surface – is almost always highly effective, as it opens the glaze for a cissing effect. It also works very well on blue and rose marbles. A cut cauliflower floret is a superb simulator of the large, branching crystals of milky white found in the pink marbles, and loaded with off-white paint or used dry to remove glaze it has few equals as a tool.

■ *Floating colour* So far we have discussed only those effects using dry grounds. Floating means marbling on a wet ground. The base colour should be dry, of course, but then a coat of flatting

MARBLING FLOORS

Wall-paints, artists' oil colours and specialized floor-paints are all suitable for floor marbling. In the case of the first two, the prime difference lies in the number of coats of protective varnish necessary – about five. Other than that, any of the techniques mentioned are suitable, with one or two logical considerations to bear in mind. For

instance, if you are going to apply a very fine, delicate marble effect, well protected by varnish, such a delicate finish is going to look very odd on floor boards where the planks are more than 1/16in (1.5mm) apart. You are never going to come across marble arranged in long, board-like slabs side by side, not to mention veins that mysteriously jump over the cracks to the next block. Either you must fill the gaps between the

board, or you must apply a much bolder, freer pattern to the marble, so that it is obviously a marble *effect* – in the same way that a book cover may be marbled – rather than an attempt at direct simulation of the real thing. Similarly, you should be careful of the colouring you choose. A bathroom or kitchen floor given a marble pattern with a white ground and blood-red veins will conjure up all sorts of gory images. On hardboard or chipboard floors, or on floorboards with the spaces well filled and sanded, the methods used for walls and other woodwork can be followed. On a floor, it is wise to use three coats of gloss or semi-gloss varnish topped by two coats of matt; this gives a sheen and a sense of depth to the colour and evokes the natural properties of marble surfaces. The darker marble finishes, such as red or serpentine, look well on floors because of their visual weight.

■ *Floor paints* Specialized floor paint is an effective marbling medium. Even its limited range of colouring is no drawback, as the colours can be inter-mixed and the muted tones are more of a help than a hindrance. There are two ways of mixing. Firstly, the base colour can be applied at full strength and the veins, thinned 1:3 mineral spirits to paint, applied with a brush or two or three feathers tied together (to cope with the thicker quality of the paint). The base colour is then applied again in the spaces between the veins and the two wet edges blended and softened together with a feather or dry brush. The alternative technique is to apply the base colour and the veins simultaneously, using one brush for each colour, and then blending the two together with a feather or dried brush. A dark grey ground with deep brick-red veins works well, or a deep red ground with grey or white veins, a white ground with grey and/or green veins, a red ground with grey or blue-green veins, black with white and green, or blue-grey with white and/or deep red veins. Coating cotton twine lines with paint and then laying them briefly on the base colour is a particularly effective method of veining on floors.

GRAINING

The practice of faking wood surfaces with paint is literally as ancient as the Egyptians and has taken many different directions over the intervening centuries. The most skilful and faithful copies, sometimes indistinguishable from the real thing, were often inspired by the shortage or high cost of the material itself, as well as by the irresistible challenge the job represented to the craftsmen. But a great number of liberties have been, and still are, taken with this technique – from stylized versions that retain the natural colourings of the wood, but discipline its random figuring into unnatural order, to fantasy versions that present the grain and other markings in a loosely realistic fashion, but depart entirely from its natural colouring.

Painted wood grain that seeks truly to deceive the eye is one of the fine arts of the decorators' craft, if that isn't a contradiction, and employs a large repertoire of techniques that can take a lifetime to learn and practise to perfection. But by acquiring just a few of these – and keeping your tongue in your cheek – you can have enormous fun creating wood-inspired finishes which, if nothing like the real thing, have definite decorative value. For those who want to try their hand at the real, representational finish, there's a chart suggesting ground and graining colours for a variety of woods. For the rest, choose colours to match your decoration scheme – safe colour bets are tone on tone, but some very pretty effects can be made with pale-to-mid-tone pastels or neutrals over a different coloured, lighter ground such as a silvery grey or beige on off-white, a cream or any of the sugar-almond colours on white, tinted with just a speck of the colour to tone. Striking contrasts often work well – black on terracotta and on emerald. Whatever combination you use, keep the ground colour several tones lighter than the graining colour so that the latter does not become overpowering. For the graining itself, it obviously helps to study the figuring of any wood you particularly like. Taking a rubbing of the grain with charcoal and paper is a useful way of isolating and becoming familiar with some of the more prominent markings. So is playing with a dry graining brush over the grain to see and feel exactly what angle and movement is needed to follow it, as well as practising the various techniques on prepainted board or paper. But don't get too perfectionist or over-intense about it; you're not training to be a master grainer and this type of decorating should, above all, be enjoyable.

■ *Materials and preparation* Graining can be done with either oil or water colour, or both. For graining in oil, use a transparent oil glaze over an eggshell ground: it's important that the ground is hard, smooth and non-absorbent, so although flat oil paint can also be used, it's worth giving it a protective coat of clear shellac or satin-finish varnish before graining. This is an essential step if you are graining on bare wood such as white-wood, and over stain on any other water-based finish, including water graining colour. This water graining colour is made in two ways, either as a 1:2 mixture of stale beer and water, or similar proportions of vinegar and water with a little sugar added to help it stick to the surface. Use powder pigments to tint it, mixing them to a smooth paste with a little of the combined liquids before adding the rest gradually, stirring them in well. This is the traditional 'cheap and cheerful' country cousin to glaze graining, although this does not dismiss its possibilities. Used sensitively, it can produce some very sophisticated results and some craftsmen prefer the special translucency of watercolour. Apart from being inexpensive, other plusses are that you can actually wash it off if you're not satisfied with the effect, providing you've sealed the ground beneath, and that it's quick drying – usually in about 15–20 minutes. This, of course, is also a disadvantage, giving you less time to work on it. It's therefore best kept for smaller or isolated areas like door panels. If it's drying too fast, you can usually brush on more of the solution without causing patchy colour and adding a few drops of glycerine will

also help slow the process down. The ground for water graining needs to have a flat finish for good adhesion. Flat oil paint or undercoat is best, sanded smooth with fine, wet-and-dry abrasive paper and soapy water. If you use eggshell paint, sand extra thoroughly to flatten the sheen and give the surface some tooth. To prevent this water-based colour cissing (forming globules) on an oil ground, rub the ground over with whiting on a damp sponge and, when dry, dust off the loose whiting powder. Adding a drop of detergent to the colour (some people actually mix the colour with hot soapy water) will also help prevent this problem. Rubbing the ground over with a soap solution just before applying the colour will help kill

any remaining grease and prevent the colour moving where you don't want it to. It's really worth experimenting with both these types of graining colour, separately and in combination, as they each have different qualities which can complement each other to produce wonderfully subtle results.

■ *Tools* The right tools – or near approximations of them – are essential for graining. Professional grainers use a whole army of specialist brushes with extraordinary names, some of them aptly descriptive like a 'mottler', which does just that to put in highlights, or a 'flogger' to beat the surface, usually to simulate pore marks. But some of them are mystifyingly obscure: why, for example, would a brush that blends and softens be called a 'badger'? Also, a 'pencil' is a brush sometimes also known as a sable writer – both names which, once you're in the know, exactly explain their fine-pointed performance. For most of the expensive, specialist brushes, the amateur can find or make adequate alternatives. If I had to choose one proper brush it would be a 'badger' softener because it can be used not only to soften and blend hard markings but to stipple, flog and even drag, too. A poor man's version is the ordinary painter's dusting brush, or 'jamb duster' whose bristles can be squared off, if

necessary, with a hammer and the blade of a craft knife.

For the rest, you will need: a medium sized decorator's brush for applying the graining colour; a graining brush – make your own from a stiff, preferably thinly bristled paintbrush by chopping the bristles off square about 1in (2.5cm) from the stock with hammer and knife-blade, as above, and cutting out clumps of bristle from each side of the brush, alternating the clumps and leaving a slight space between them; a graining comb – cut irregularly spaced notches out of a piece of strong cardboard or

ABOVE *A room full of character, but all of it superimposed and at a fraction of the cost of real wood panelling and custom-made cupboards. What makes this room work is scrupulous attention to detail and a degree of restraint. The walls and cupbards are trimmed and panelled with moulding, the likely direction of real grain faithfullly adhered to on each section, and joins are shown clearly as they would be on the real thing. The graining itself is kept simple and the areas of patterning well-spaced.*

BELOW *Simple graining*
1 A coat of glaze is laid over the ground and dragged with a dry brush to give a basic texture.
2 Combing inserts more definitive straight grain.
3 A fitch is used to fidget in the outline of the heart wood.
4 A method of adding knots – rag-covered forefinger placed straight down on the glaze and then turned, as if trying to press in a drawing pin.

1

2

3

4

plastic (for regularly spaced grain, buy a cheap metal comb, which will also be useful for separating the bristles of the graining brush); make a knot tool by notching a cork or coring the centre bristles from a stencil brush and removing clumps around the edges; a wide, soft-bristled paintbrush will serve for mottling and, at a pinch, for softening and blending too; a fine-pointed artists' sable brush is useful for teasing out, or in, individual lines of grain; back-up equipment could include a marine sponge, chamois leather and clean rags.

■ *Method* The character of every species of wood is basically defined by its colour, grain, pore marking and mottling. In painted versions there's no need to even attempt to interpret these accurately, as long as they are combined in a form which roughly represents the natural texture of wood and the rhythm of its figuring. If you look at a piece of wood, you'll see that there is a definite pacing of the markings, but that they are never exactly evenly spaced nor exactly repetitive. Notice how the grain changes from light to dark, thick to thin, wide-spread to closely spaced, straight to curved; smooth-edged to jagged or blurred in outline; how it is stronger and darker as it curves around the knot and becomes straighter and fainter as it veers away from it; how it gets broader and spacier as it curves again into the long, ragged oval shape of the heartwood. In painted versions, you can place all these separate elements in a form to suit you and the surface you're working on – just try to keep a balance between the absolutely regular, which would look unnatural, and the absolutely random, which would look equally unrealistic and aesthetically unpleasing. The following sequence of methods will give you one kind of woody impression, but by experimenting with each one and with different combinations and in different sequences, you will find that a considerable variety of effects can be

obtained with the same basic collection of tools and techniques.

Texture Brush on the glaze and then rake it through from edge to edge with a dry graining brush; for a heavier texture, rake it through again with a comb. In both cases, undulate the graining tool slightly from side to side as you draw it

RIGHT *Fine, darker lines emphasize joins and, brushed and blotted in moulding recesses, prevent panels looking too brash and new by suggesting the natural build-up of a little dust in the appropriate crevices.*

down the surface to give the grain a gently waving quality.

Pore marks Hold the dry dusting brush – or the flogger if you have one – almost horizontal to the surface and beat it lightly all over, as if you were using a carpetbeater. Beating with the grain will produce one effect, against the grain another. An alternative method for introducing pore marks is to hold the dusting brush perpendicular to the surface and stipple it all over or push it backwards and forwards over the grain

to break it up, beating it afterwards against the grain with a dry brush to soften the markings. For a different type of pore marking, protect the otherwise completed finish with a coat of clear shellac, then spatter a fine spray of colour lightly over the surface and soften it by whisking it immediately with

the bristle-tips of a soft, dry brush in the direction of the grain. Experiment with these methods and take your pick.

Mottling Mottles are the silvery highlights that run across the grain to give may woods a satiny sheen. Again, here are two methods which each produce a different effect. Either fold a chamois leather, dampened with mineral spirits or water (depending on whether you're using an oil or water graining colour) and roll it down the surface; or dampen the bristles of a clean brush with the wet chamois, rest them lightly across the grain and rock the brush from side to side. In this way you can take the colour off in irregular, horizontal patches down the surface; overlap each patch to avoid getting regular, vertical divisions, which do not do anything for the finish.

and, whether you're using the brush wet or dry, play with its versatility. Changing pressure will alter the marks it makes from narrow to broad, close- to wide-spaced. This is particularly useful for putting in rings where, by varying the position, pressure and direction of the brush, you can move from dense, dark

pointed artists' brush, the edge of a cork or with your thumb nail wrapped in clean rag. On different woods, the grain is jagged or smooth; for a jagged effect, just wobble the tool gently as you draw it through the colour. When the patterning is in, soften and blend hard lines by lightly whisking across the surface along the grain with the bristle-tips of a soft, dry brush. This will give a much more authentic end result.

▌ *Finishing off* Graining done in the water medium will need two or three coats of clear varnish for protection. Oil glaze, while less vulnerable, is also more durable under varnish and you may, anyway, want to use a tinted varnish to mellow the surface.

BEER AND VINEGAR GRAINING

Either oil or watercolour paints can be used for graining and beer or vinegar mixed with water is probably the cheapest version of the watercolours. The ground for this technique needs to have a flat finish, so flat-oil paint or undercoat is best, sanded down with wet-and-dry abrasive paper and soapy water. This sanding should be carefully and thoroughly done on eggshell paint to ensure good adhesion and to flatten the sheen. The chief problem with using watercolour on an oil ground is that globules of water tend to form on the surface rather than spreading in an even film. For this reason, it's advisable to run over an oil ground with whiting on a damp sponge and then dust off the loose whiting powder when dry. Rubbing the ground with soap solution will also help to eliminate grease spots that will otherwise cause colour to ciss.

Stale beer – preferably brown ale because of its high sugar content – mixed at a 1:2 beer to water ratio, is capable of giving a variety of shades from deep amber to pale gold when applied with a brush. Malt or red wine vinegar and water at the same 1:2 ratio gives a slightly redder tone (don't use

LEFT *Knowing when to stop is so important. The lining and shelves in this corner cupboard, sponged in a watery blue on cream to set off the blue and old-white china, makes a refreshing change.*

FAR LEFT *One of the advantages of graining over real wood is that you can choose where knots appear and use them for decorative interest.*

Knots These are put in with the cored stencil brush or notched cork by placing the end squared against the surface and twisting it. The surface may then be grained again to show stronger markings curving round the knots and straightening out between them. The stronger, darker markings can also be painted in with a fine-pointed artists' brush. The graining brush can also, of course, be used to put colour on as well as taking it off. Separate the bristles with a comb after loading it with colour

grain at one side to broad, widely spaced grain at the top of the curve before it narrows and tightens again on the other side. This can be done in one movement, with the process repeated to fill in the bottom half of the ring. Feather joins with a dry brush, so that they are unobtrusive and well finished off.
Heartwood These are the sets of distinctive, concentric ovals that sometimes contain a knot and sometimes do not. For these you can take the colour off either with a fine-

1

2

3

4

onion vinegar – it is too pale); it is a good idea to add a little sugar to this solution to help it stick to the surface – about 2tsp:1pt (10gm:600ml). Either mixture can be tinted with powder pigments by mixing the pigment to a smooth paste with a little of the beer/water or vinegar/water mixture first and then gradually stirring them into the main body of liquid.

These beer or vinegar stain/paints have a translucency that can give a remarkably sophisticated finish if they are used with care. In fact, the sap that produces wood grain is not dissimilar in consistency. The softness of the colours also means that they can be strengthened with additional brush strokes without building up a sticky layering, which is what tends to occur when thickening other types of paint. They can be blurred softly along the edges with a damp sponge, and it is even possible to evoke the ragged ovals of heartwood by laying on a long oval area of water with a sponge and then coasting a brush loaded with beer or vinegar stain down each edge. The inside edge of the stain stroke should haze and blend, fading in toward the centre of the oval. The other grains can be applied with an artists' brush, from 1/16in (0.15cm) upward, a ½in (1.2cm) being about the best general width for washing in between the grains, and a ¼in (0.6cm) the most suitable for the grains themselves.

■ *Application* There are two main methods for beer or vinegar graining. The first has much to do with the basic techniques of all watercolour painting, and the second with dragging. The watercolour approach involves drawing in the grain lines with a brush, in the same manner as you would use a pencil; a sign-writers' brush, known as a pencil writer, is highly effective for this. Load the brush to about a third of the way along the hairs, but not so much that it drips. Holding it as you would the shaft of a pen, rest the tip on the surface and, in a continuous movement, draw the

brush downward; the good news is that you don't have to worry about wobbling, but try not to let the stroke appear 'tight' – full of little kinks. This will happen if you hold the brush too tightly and go too slowly. It is best to practise on some paper first. If you wish to soften one side of a piece of grain, either take a larger brush, dampened but not dripping, and tease the edge of the grain stroke; alternatively you could lay a stroke of water down the surface before you make the grain stroke and let the grain line follow along the edge of the wet area. Keep a sponge handy at all times. Knots can be simulated by laying a circular patch of colour on the surface and pressing a dry, notched cork immediately into the wet area, or a torn, screwed knot of blotting paper, which is often more effective.

There are two great assets to this method, besides being inexpensive. First, it dries very quickly – in about 15–20 minutes, which means you can touch it up without worrying about smudging the parts that you have already done; and second, it can be washed off immediately after application if you haven't got what you want, although for this it is essential that you've sealed the surface first. Some people consider the quick drying a drawback, because you may not achieve the desired effect before it dries; but this scarcely matters since you can still wash it off when dry. In any case, you can slow the drying time by adding a few drops of glycerine. Probably the prime limitation of this medium is its delicacy; like so much watercolour work, it looks best fairly small. To undertake a very large area can make the effect appear too fragile for the space, so it is best to stick to door panels and small, inset areas.

It is absolutely essential to protect watercolour of this type with at least two coats of clear, semi-gloss varnish, otherwise it can easily wash off or wear away.

LEFT *Sequence for mahogany*
1 *A red-brown paint is applied and stirred in sweeping swirls, using a soft dragger.*
2 *Darker, burnt umber grain swirls follow the pattern, applied either with a dragger or with a fine brush, using a scribbling or shading stroke.*
3 *A short dragger gives a silky ripple to the grain.*
4 *The whole surface is softened with a badger softener.*

1

2

3

4

5

ABOVE *Sequence for simulating bird's eye maple.*
1 A generous paint glaze is laid over the ground and a series of rhythmic crinkles achieved by using the end of a soft rubber comb, pressing right down, then releasing sharply upward.
2 This effect is softened with a badger softener.
3 The 'bird's eyes' are blotted in the wet glaze with a fingertip.

4 The eyes are joined with a soft pencil in the manner of grains.
5 The result is a highly stylized version of this maple.

TORTOISESHELL

As a decorative medium, real and simulated tortoiseshell originated in the Far East, with the first costly examples reaching Europe in the seventeenth century. The great majority of these were small and exquisitely prepared: panels mounted in ivory or ebony, small lacquered boxes or toilet utensils. Soon, tortoiseshell's distinctive colouring, markings and opulent appearance made it a prominent feature in the craze for 'things oriental' that subsequently swept Europe. Cabinet-makers and decorators were not slow to reproduce its appearance on objects ranging from lacquered furniture to cornices and ceilings – where it appeared in the form of inset oval and circular panels. For the most part, these areas were kept small; this was partly an aesthetic decision and partly due to the medium required – varnish. Varnish is essential for tortoiseshelling, but it tends to dry quickly, making it almost obligatory to restrict the finish to small areas. The limited size of the original examples meant that they could be sumptuously exotic. European craftsmen of the period soon realized this and, although they rarely achieved the finesse of their oriental counterparts, whose varnishes were long perfected for this use, they often showed greater variety and innovation, while taking care not to apply excessively large areas of this exotic shell patterning.

Bearing all this in mind may help you to avoid making the worst aesthetic mistake possible with tortoiseshell: applying too much of it over large areas as if it were marble, or over areas of intricately curved and convoluted mouldings or heavy furniture, where real tortoiseshell could never have been used. Such an error of judgement results in transforming a beautiful, often jewel-like mottle into a disastrously vulgar absurdity.

The natural colouring of tortoiseshell varies from golden honey tones through the tawny auburns to an almost fire-ember red. Even so, like marbling, the term tortoiseshell has come to describe a particular type of paint finish, a patterning and use of paint and varnish in the manner of tortoiseshell but without necessarily being an exact copy of the real thing. Tortoiseshell can, for example, mean imposing markings of deep brown or red-chestnut over a deep blue or emerald. In this way it may even resemble the patterns found on butterfly wings.

The scale of the patterning you use should be most influenced by the size of the area you intend to paint, and that area should be either a flat or a gently curved surface, not one with a high relief or mouldings. Because the technique involves brushing patches of oil paint into wet varnish it is very difficult for one person to tortoiseshell a large area – which is just as well, as it prevents invidiously large-scale execution with excessive results. If tortoiseshell is chosen for a large wall, it

is wise to divide the area into panels – no larger than 3ft (90cm) – and to execute the panels alternately so that each has its own identity, rather than creating one big spread, which will look awful. Two people can do the job more speedily than one but remember that (as with shading and stippling), each person has a distinctly different touch, so either one person should always apply the varnish and the other brush the paint into it, or they should each work on their own separate panel section. If you decide to divide a wall into panels, divide it first with chalk lines, then put masking tape down the edges of each area. Paint the panels alternately, leaving every second panel blank; when the first set is dry, paint the others, removing the masking tape when you've completed both sets. Paint the areas between the panels afterwards, using masking tape along the edges.

If you intend to work on a door, it is often useful to remove it from its hinges and lay it down flat. Doors are a prime

example of where and where not, and how and how not to apply tortoiseshell. If the door is panelled, it is very unwise – and very unsuccessful – to tortoiseshell the entire surface. It will simply look silly and ugly because the panels and raised areas together will bear no relation to the patterns of the tortoiseshell. However, if you paint only the inset panels – and they are small, plentiful and regularly spaced – it can look very handsome. A flush door can look superb. It is also possible to simulate the kind of surrounds that were occasionally used to frame tortoiseshell: metal, ivory and ebony. Ivory can be simulated by an Indian yellow and flake white oil paint covered with two coats of varnish – a matt coat over a gloss coat – both tinted to a pale amber. Ebony can be evoked with burnt umber and lampblack, given two coats of varnish – matt over gloss – both tinted with a trace of red.

Whichever way you may choose to evoke tortoiseshell, always remember

LEFT *One would not readily imagine that this very stylish side cupboard could be finished just by mottling its tinted glaze with a folded cloth and then softening the effect with a dry brush.*

that it is an opulent, exotic effect. It works well on flat details in bathrooms, intimate halls, dressing rooms or bedrooms, on furniture – especially the tops of small decorative side-tables – and ornamental objects. Like marble, it should not be applied to a surface that could never have been made of tortoiseshell in the first place, or to which a panel of credible size could not have been fitted. Giant tortoises may be substantial creatures but no elephant-sized ones have been located to date.

GOLDEN TORTOISESHELL

This is probably the lightest of the realistic tortoiseshell effects, essentially a blond rather than auburn finish. It gives a sensation of less weight and can therefore be executed over a slightly larger area.

■ **Materials** The ground or base coat should be an eggshell or low-lustre oil-based paint in a light, warm, sandy yellow. Tinted varnish is essential: either dark oak thinned 1:1 with mineral spirits, or light oak. On plaster, varnish is better unthinned, so it is preferable to use undiluted light oak; on wood, thinned varnish is more effective. Two dark brown artists' oil colours, raw and burnt umber; two ordinary paint brushes, one for wet varnish, the other to be used dry, sizes 2–5in (5–10cm); two artists' brushes about ½in (1.2cm) in width; mineral spirits, clean rags and cotton batting are also necessary.

■ **Application** It is a very good idea to have a look at a sample of real or simulated tortoiseshell, in either a museum or publication, before attempting to reproduce it. It does have a very distinctive appearance, but is subtle and various for all that, and by no means repetitive.

The base coat should be applied and allowed to dry. Then, before varnish is applied, the tinting oil colours should be prepared with a little mineral spirits. The movement of tortoiseshell, like marble, is diagonal and slightly

radiating, so that bands of colour diverge. To achieve this effect, use one of the two broader brushes, and apply the varnish quickly and liberally over the base coat, moving diagonally from the top right (unless you are left-handed, in which case start at the top left) down over the whole area of the panel. Then, using the same brush, work or tease the varnish into a series of diagonal bands of zig-zag direction and irregular width. At this point, take either a screwed-up rag or a piece of cotton batting soaked in mineral spirits and fray the edges of the varnish bands so that they will be receptive to paint blending. Now, before the varnish sets, work the lighter of the two prepared oil colours into the gaps between the bands of varnish with one of the two artists' brushes. For this, use either a flat, zig-zag motion – as if you were shading with a pencil or wax crayon – or roll the brush-tip over the surface of the varnish. Then insert the darker brown into the centre of the light with the other small brush.

Once you have applied these colours, soften their edges into the varnish by stroking the whole surface very gently with the other large brush, which you should have kept clean and dry for this purpose. Go in the same direction as that of the dark patterns; then cross off vertically, and finish off by going in the original diagonal direction again. You can repeat this procedure as often as you like until you get a soft finish that satisfies you, but always remember that the final diagonal should be in the direction in which you originally applied the varnish.

This is the most basic tortoiseshell technique, but you can add as many accents and flourishes as you like. Flecks or freckles often occur in tortoiseshell along the lines of the main marks, but set at a slight angle to them, rather as pine needles radiate along the general line of a twig – only, of course, much more sparsely. Fill an eye-dropper with mineral spirits or wood alcohol and

1

4

Sequence for golden tortoiseshell
1 *A tinted varnish is brushed over a cream ground and irregular Indian red patches twirled into it simultaneously.*
2 *These are crossed and blended.*
3 *Indian red and burnt sienna patches are teased into the varnish with an artists' brush.*
4 *Blend with a swift crossing stroke.*
5 *The whole is softened by criss-crossing with a wide, dry brush.*

2

3

let spots fall sparsely on the varnish. This cissing will open the varnish and into the resulting holes you can insert a small spot of the darker oil colour as soon as the cissing has dried. Augment the cissing with small, dark spots of oil colour and then drop a spot of the solvent into these to create rings, or eyes. When these eyes have dried, you can add a tiny spot in the centre of them, if you like this effect. Alternatively, you can fray the edges of the bands or spots of oil colour in the same manner, and leave the cissing spots unfilled if you choose.

AUBURN TORTOISESHELL

This is a rich, red-chestnut tortoiseshell, reminiscent of the tawny wings of the tortoiseshell butterfly.

▐ **Materials** A base of brick-red mixed 1:1 with yellow ochre a dark oak varnish and two artists' oil colours – lampblack and burnt umber – are necessary to apply the finish, in addition to those brushes and tools previously mentioned.

▐ **Application** Over the base coat, apply a dark oak varnish, using the same type of stroke as you would for golden tortoiseshell. Before applying the oil colour, mix some of the varnish with the lampblack, 2:1 paint to varnish or, if you prefer it paler, 1:1. Use this mix to insert the first, broader, diagonal paint strokes in the usual manner. Then brush a mix of lampblack and burnt umber into these, concentrating the deeper tones at the centre. Blend the paint and varnish with the dry brush as normal, and then, in patches along the line of the main paint marks, ciss the varnish to your taste; make sure that the cissing occurs just alongside the paint marks but not over them. Fill the cissing with black or burnt umber.

A darker, red version of this variant uses a solid, brick-red ground, dark oak varnish and lampblack oil colour; its method of application is the same, mixing varnish with oil colour in a ratio of 2:1 for the initial dark strokes.

5

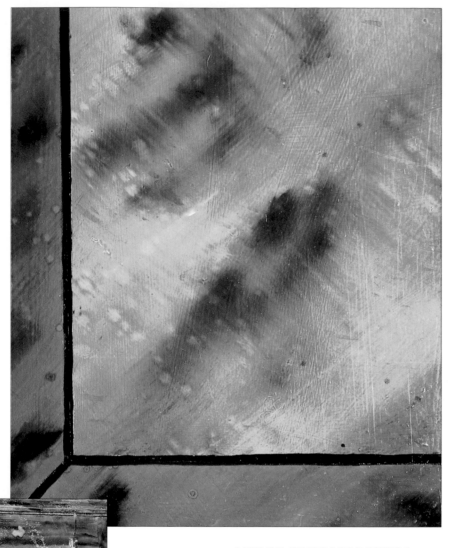

black. If the dark paint areas are smaller, the raw umber need not be diluted but simply brushed into the varnish in the conventional manner, with the lampblack used in the centre. Cissing in the centre of dark paint spots – to make rings – works well on this version, as gentler contrast prevents the softness of the rings from being overshadowed by other elements.

FINISHING OFF

Absolutely never use matt varnish to give a top protective coat to tortoiseshell; it kills the light-reflective quality in the paint/varnish. Strictly speaking, it isn't really necessary to put on a top varnish coat at all, as the technique is essentially a paint/varnish one anyway, but real tortoiseshell has a sheen like silk. A semi-gloss polyurethane varnish is effective, but the most accurate and perhaps the most pleasing way to finish tortoiseshell on woodwork is to sand down the polyurethane top coat with a very fine wet-and-dry paper, used with a solution of water and mild soap-flakes. Then polish this with a solution of rotten-stone and warm linseed oil, mixed to a paste.

BAMBOO

Bamboo is another example of a technique where, although it's as helpful, informative and inspirational as ever to study the original, nature is only the beginning of the painted art. As long as the two basic styles are loosely adhered to – that is, the typical patterning of male and female bamboo – fantasy can take over at any stage of this technique and, used with imagination and taste, prove stunningly effective.

To the Chinese, the bamboo has always been both a decorative inspiration and a practical material for the construction of buildings and furniture, but it wasn't until the seventeenth century that the

ABOVE *Painted golden tortoiseshell panel with painted auburn tortoiseshell border. The lighter area has patches of blue brushed into it as well as burnt umber, and cissing spots splashed on after the finish has been crossed with a dry brush.*

LEFT *The entire surface of this panelled door has been tortoiseshelled – a treatment which may be a little extreme for some tastes, but is obviously not intended to look realistic.*

AMBER TORTOISESHELL

This is a warm, golden-tinged effect, deeper than the honey-blond tones and less red than auburn. It has the same visual weight as mid-oak panelling.
▌ *Materials* The base colour should be yellow ochre and the varnish dark oak. The two oil colours are raw umber and lampblack.
▌ *Application* If you intend to use a large, dark, zig-zag pattern with this tortoiseshell, you may want to thin the oil paint in varnish for the initial paint shading after the application of the main varnish coat. If you do this, the undiluted raw umber should form the centre of the zig-zag with a trace of

burgeoning China trade brought its possibilities home to Europeans. Since it was initially too expensive for those other than well-heeled high society, craftsmen literally 'turned' to copying it in wood and these turned and decorated pieces became an art in themselves, reaching the peak of popularity in the eighteenth century when they were painted not only in subtle colours to simulate the natural material, but in brilliant hued fantasy versions, too. The fashion for real bamboo was revived in Victorian and Edwardian times often decoratively scorched rather than painted – and it is furniture from these periods, that most often turns up in junk shops, ripe for renovation. But the decorative features of bamboo can be used just as effectively on other surfaces around the home as it can on furniture, making a very pretty treatment for any suitably rounded picture or mirror frames, or woodwork mouldings such as those on architraves or the balusters along staircases and landings. To prevent it looking silly, the distinctive markings of the female bamboo, which has dark spines and 'eyes' as well as the knotty joints, should only be painted either on real bamboo or on turned wood that echoes its shape, even if not exactly simulating it. The simpler, tone-on-tone ring markings of the male bamboo can be used on any type of round mouldings – and these can also be added to the 'female' type for effect. Colours are really up to you: dark on light, woody colours to simulate the real thing, pastels on white or off-white for a pale and pretty effect, different tones of the same colour for subtlety or brilliant colours and dramatic contrasts for drama and sophistication. The 'female' bamboo figuring generally looks best if the knots, spines and eye centres are painted in the same colour and one which is darker than the ground but, again, these conventions can be broken with impunity: you might, for example, use a mid-grey for knots, spines and eyes on a black ground, dotting in the eye-

LEFT AND ABOVE
Real bamboo can be embellished with paint to bring out the distinctive details – thin, parallel rings for male bamboo; dark spines and eyes for female bamboo.

centres alternately with black and scarlet. It is really entirely up to individual taste and preference.

■ *Preparation* If you are merely adding decoration to natural bamboo, give it a preliminary wash with methylated spirits to remove any grease or oil, and any old French polish. If you are both painting and decorating bamboo, wash as above before applying at least three coats of thinned flat oil paint or undercoat, sanding carefully between coats with fine, wet-and-dry abrasive paper and soapy water. If you're working on turned wood, you can leave out the wash (although a quick rub over with either methylated or mineral spirits is always a worthwhile safety precaution against grease on previously painted surfaces) and paint as above. Whatever ground you're working on, protect it with a coat of thinned, clear matt varnish or shellac; this will not only seal surface porosity but enable you to quickly wipe off any decorative mistakes with the appropriate solvent before they

RIGHT *Decorative treatment for bamboo can vary from picking out realistic features to more fantastic treatments. A length of real bamboo can be a useful source of ideas, but nature need not be copied slavishly.*

dry. It is certainly worth taking the trouble to achieve a smooth ground coat, as delicate decoration will not only be difficult to achieve and wasted on a rough ground, it will also serve to emphasize surface imperfections; so do take the trouble with the ground coat.

■ *Materials* Although you can use flat oil paint, thinned to the consistency of cream and tinted with universal stainers, for decoration , these take so long to dry that an otherwise delicate and delightful job can become a bore. The quick-drying signwriters' colours are ideal, as are artists' acrylic colours; thin these to a creamy consistency with mineral spirits or water respectively, so that you get colour that is smooth-flowing yet still opaque. For the subtle, more naturalistic and near-transparent ring markings of male bamboo, use 'sharp' colour – that is, artists' oil colour dissolved in a little mineral spirits, mixed with varnish and then further thinned with solvent. You'll need three tones – the darkest one for the knot, plus two paler ones. Mix the lightest, most transparent tone, first, thinning the varnish about 1:1 with solvent and get the two darker tones by adding more colour and more varnish, using about half the amount of solvent to varnish for the mid-tone and a 4:1 mixture of varnish and solvent for the darker of the tones.

■ *Tools* You will need two ordinary paintbrushes for stripping the male bamboo, one ¾in (1.9cm) and one 1in (2.5cm), and two fine-pointed artists' sable brushes – a No 3 and No 6 are the most versatile combination – for the decorative detailing.

■ *Method* *Female bamboo* With the No 3 sable brush, paint in the knots between the bamboo sections, pressing the brush so that the paint extends up and over about 1/16in (1.5mm) of the rings at each side of the knot (the rings look like lips in profile, so it's easy to see where the 'lipstick' should stop). Paint in the spines in the same colour. These start from each knot as two lines about

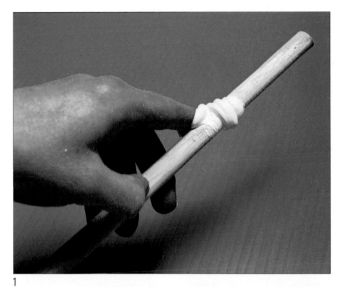

1

2

3

4

¼–⅜in (6–9mm) apart and curve
towards each other to meet and form
one straight line, which tapers to a point
as you gently lighten the pressure on the
brush. The spines can vary in length, but
traditionally never extend more than
one-third of the length of the section

and, where there are two spines
pointing away from a knot, it looks
better if their bases overlap or just
touch rather than being absolutely
symmetrical. The open area between the
two branches of the spine can also be
filled in with colour if you wish. Next to
be added are the eyes, using light but
firm pressure with the No 6 brush to
create slightly oval dots of colour,
usually in a mid-tone which contrasts
with both knots/spines and ground.
When these are dry, use the No 3 brush
and the knot/spine colour to place a tiny
dot off-centre in each eye and two or
three dots around it. The placing of both
eyes and dots is important: the eyes
should be near enough to the spines to
relate to them, but randomly spaced to
create a more lively effect, and the dots
should relate to the eyes in the same
way, placed usually in singles or pairs,
but with their formation changing from
eye to eye.

Male bamboo Apply sufficient pressure
on the ordinary ¾in (1.9cm) brush,
using the thinnest, palest of the colours
(see above), to paint in an even,
translucent band which is centred on
the knot and extends about ½in (1.2cm)
each side of it. When this is dry, add
enough colour and varnish to this
mixture to thicken and darken it to a
mid-tone and, with the 1in (2.5cm)
brush, paint a second, narrower ring
over the first, again centred over the
knot. Add more varnish and more colour
to make your darkest tone to paint in
the knot with the No 3 artists' brush, as
for the female bamboo above.

■ *Additions and variations* The knots
on female bamboo can be further
emphasized with a single broad band of
translucent colour, as in the lightest of
the stripes for male bamboo. The
sections between the knots can be
lightly dragged with toning or
contrasting colour before the detailing is
painted on or, after decoration, the
entire piece can be brushed and/or
dragged with tinted varnish or antiqued
by any method, including freckling the

area either side of each knot with a fine spattering of paint in the same tone. A fantasy version of male bamboo can be achieved by striping the whole length of the shaft with rings in a contrasting colour to the ground: use the No 3 and No 6 brush to vary both the width and spacing of the rings for a random effect, or paint on the second colour all over and comb the rings on, either straight or in jagged zig-zags. Real fantasy female bamboo can be achieved by retaining the positioning of spines and eyes but replacing the traditional figuring with a suitable pattern of your own choice, such as leaves and flowers of some description.

■ *Finishing touches* Whichever treatment you use, wait until the decoration is completely dry before adding two or more coats of clear varnish. Painted pieces will look better under matt varnish, satin will most resemble the natural sheen of real bamboo while gloss may be needed to bring out brilliant colours and give a lacquer-like finish to fantasy pieces. These are useful hints on the best finishing treatments if you are unsure of yourself.

ANTIQUING

To age an object all in a moment, look at it with half-closed eyes. Squint your eyes at a wall and its colour dims; furnishings blur slightly, their sharp edges round. There are many techniques that will achieve this artificial ageing, with paint offering some of the most versatile and straightforward methods. Many ageing methods are really extensions of spattering, colour washing and stippling, which have already been described so all that it is necessary to explain here is how they are used in a specific, softening way. The tools and equipment are the same, too, and it is simply a re-use of colour and some care – and logic – that is needed when using these tools to simulate or stress age.

The first thing to remember in antiquing either a wall or a wooden surface is that age dims a shine and takes the edge off colour. That doesn't mean it kills it – indeed, it may improve it considerably – but remember that what you should aim to achieve is an after-glow, a sunset on the surface, not a cloudy night. Using paint and paint glazes, there are three main techniques open to you: glazing and spattering on woodwork and colour-washing on walls.

WOODWORK

■ *Glazing* Paint glazes or oil glazes are among the most versatile antiquing approaches on woodwork, oil glazes offering the greater translucency. A 3:1 mixture of paint to matt varnish, tinting the paint first by mixing it with oil glaze, gives a high degree of transparency with a delicate, non-reflective finish. The chief difference between this and a straight oil glaze is that any glaze mixed with varnish cannot be rubbed or wiped when it is touch dry, while oil or paint glazes can. Therefore, for a wiping technique you have to use varnish-free glazes, either clear or tinted, and you can use them separately or together. If you use tinted and untinted varnish with a blending technique, lay the clear glaze on to the centre of the area and then, with a stippling motion, brush the tinted glaze into it from the edges. On mouldings it is easier to use a single, tinted glaze, apply it overall, and then rub the glaze off the raised areas with a cloth wrung out in mineral spirits, leaving the glaze gathered in the crevices. Then stipple it to kill any hard edges. If you use a tinted glaze over a flat area like a table, wipe from the centre and blend with a stippling brush toward the edges. If you want a light effect, it is useful to allow the glaze to dry at least overnight and then rub it from the centre with fine steel wool and blend it softly, leaving the edges darker. Then apply a second, thinned coat over that to give it a softer appearance.

RIGHT *Antiquing. Beams here have two coats of thinned, white paint, sanded off to show the wood. Walls have a white distemper and buff wash.*

The colours used in antiquing wood are similar to those of graining. In almost all cases they are the earth colours – burnt umber, burnt sienna and lampblack. A black surface is the only exception to this, where the antiquing colours should be dark brown.

▮ *Spattering* Spattering is the key to evoking those 'fly-specks' like freckles on an elderly face that typify so much old, polished woodwork. The most effective medium for this form of spattering is either artists' oil colour or brown or black ink. In the case of ink, coat the surface first with shellac or varnish, and then apply the spatters in the usual way. With antiquing, the thing to note is *where* to spatter. Choose the places where the tiny gashes that collect dirt and old polish usually occur as these ultimately cause fly-specks – on the edges of drawers, the edges of level tops and surfaces, the tops and edges of raised turnings on banisters or furniture legs. Fly-specks do not usually gather on the flat, central planes, except here and there in a linear string, where any spattering should be much smudged and finely spread. Generally, don't make the spatters too regular, and vary their size. Blot or stipple the surface and if you want to, ciss it with water over the ink or whisk the spatters with a soft, dry brush before the ink or paint sets. You can also reduce overdone areas with steel wool. Then varnish over the top of the spatter layer.

On wood surfaces, always bear in mind that a gloss varnish produces a harsh surface that looks totally wrong over antiquing. At most, you should apply a soft, satin sheen. This can be achieved by using several coats of thinned clear matt or satin varnish or polyurethane and, if you wish, tint that to a mellow tone.

WALLS

■ *Colour-washing and glazing* The main target in ageing a wall surface is to soften it, not darken the colour. Walls that aren't flat and can't be made so – like many in older buildings – benefit from a matt colour wash. A very thin wash should be used on them. The paler blues soften with a thin, raw umber wash. A grey wall can be warmed by raw or burnt umber either separately or together, touched with a spot of black. Green surfaces need a slightly deeper green that can be cooled down with raw umber or warmed up with burnt umber. White walls need a very thin wash of burnt umber, and the same goes for off-white, beiges, dusty pinks and yellows.

For level wall surfaces, oil glazes work very well. Their translucence tinted delicately with the oil colours listed above, gives a patina of diffused softness that cannot be achieved solely with a paint wash.

PORPHYRY

Porphyry is an igneous rock whose granitic texture comes from the many minerals embedded in its fine-grained mass. Although its name comes from the Greek word for 'purple' and was originally used to describe a particular reddish-purple and white variety, often used for sculpture because its hard surface can be given an almost glass-like polish, porphyry is now used much more loosely to cover a whole family of this rock-type, members of which are found in many different colourings. Other typical combinations are: brown, veined with near-transparent white and flecked with pink, red and green; dark green flecked with gold and black; violet flecked with gold, black and iron grey; reddish brown flecked with light brown and black or with reddish purple, black and pale pink. It is always worth studying the originals for information and inspiration for decorative purposes, as with the other techniques, but considerable artistic license may also be taken with colour combinations as long as the characteristic granite-like texture is observed. This is easily represented by spattering a sequence of watery colours over a plain or sponged ground. The recipe given is for a grey-green porphyry with distinctive flecks of off-white and black, but with the technique at your fingertips, the colours can be varied to suit your taste.

■ *Materials* The ground colour requires a white flat oil paint or undercoat, tinted to a beige-grey with artists' oil colours in raw umber and pale yellow ochre (proportions are roughly one part of each oil colour to six parts of paint). Make enough of this mix so that, together with some of the plain white oil paint, it may also be used for the spattering coats. For the spattering colours, make up six different shades from the paint, artists' oil colours and mineral spirits.

The first three evolve from the ground colour, one being the same, one lightened with a little white and the third darkened a roughly equal degree with a little black. Then make up a slightly off-white shade by adding a speck of raw umber to the white paint. For the fifth colour, add to some of this off-white enough pale yellow ochre and green chromium oxide to make a pale, milky, yellowy green. The last colour is simply the black artists' oil colour, dissolved in mineral spirits. All colours are thinned to the consistency of skimmed milk with mineral spirits (above 1:3 mixture of paint and solvent).

■ *Method* Apply two coats of ground colour and, when they are dry, sand down with fine abrasive paper to provide a tooth. Then spatter all over with each of the colours in turn in the same sequence as they are given above, but waiting for each spattering to dry before adding the next. Bear in mind that porphyry often shows drifts of different crystals, so there is no need to try to achieve a uniform dispersal of each colour. Similarly, although most of the spattering should be finely sprayed, passing knife or finger across the loaded bristle-tips of the brush, it looks more natural if there are occasionally larger and more irregular dots of paint. For these, knock the stock of the loaded brush against a block of wood, which will release larger, different-sized particles of paint. You can vary size and texture still further by adding a little more solvent to the paint. The finest spray of all with be achieved by using a diffuser, bought from artists' suppliers. This extremely basic piece of equipment – simply two short, slim tubes connected at a right angle – relies on one of the fundamental laws of physics to produce a remarkably sophisticated result: by resting the end of one tube in a jar of water colour and blowing through the other end, a vacuum is created which draws the colour up to the top of the first tube; one further puff will spray it onto the surface.

For this particuar, very granite-like porphyry effect, keep the spattering of greys fairly regular, with just a few lighter and darker areas, using the knife- (or finger-) across-brush technique. Use brush-against-block to spatter the off-white, making freckles of a more random size and in a sparser arrangement; spatter the green in fine, hazy drifts – ideally with a diffuser – and use a mixture of the first two techniques for the final, light spattering of black.

■ *Finishing off* Protect porphyry finishes with two coats of clear varnish. Whether to use matt, satin finish or gloss depends on preference and surface – you may, for example, want a matt, more stone-like finish for walls. For a more reflective finish, apply enough coats of gloss to level the surface. This should give a high enough shine to obviate polishing, which could unsettle the fragile surface.

TRANSLUCENT
AND
TRANSPARENT
FINISHES

STAINING

Staining is an alternative to paint in the decorative treatment of woodwork. The prime reason for using a stain is because being tinted with dyes rather than pigments, the various media used remain translucent, so that the wood can be coloured without obscuring its texture or grain. Staining is also quicker, and often cheaper than painting, but among the reasons why it's not more popular is, of course, that it doesn't cover a mixture of surfaces or a multitude of imperfections with the same *sang-froid*; although staining can do much to perk up a piece of rather plain wood, the smooth, sound, uniform, clean surface must already be there. Another reason more people don't use stain is because they don't realize the wide range of both colours and types available. Most shops only stock a very limited range and usually only in the 'natural' wood shades (often in the very ill-formulated varnish stains, usually made from oil stain mixed with gloss varnish, which leave a nasty sludge on the surface), plus a few bright colours, if you're lucky. Yet just a little investigation will discover water stains, spirit stains, oil stains, even wax stains. Some are ready mixed in solution form,

some come as crystals to be mixed with water or spirit (usually methylated spirit). There is a considerable range of colours, which can in themselves be blended (although not, obviously, between different stain types), some manufacturers will make up colours to order, or match colour samples, and you can make up your own wood-dyes from the standard range of textile dyes sold in the shops.

Water stains This type of stain has several advantages: it usually fades less noticeably than other types, it is inexpensive and it forms an even colour with relative ease. Ready mixed colour ranges can be slightly dull, but it is simple enough to make your own from the powder textile dyes, giving you access to a considerable range of clear, bright colours. Follow the manufacturer's instructions for dissolving the dye but, for staining, use about half as much water as they suggest. Test colours out on spare pieces of a similar wood before applying and be prepared to apply two or more coats before the colour really begins to show. The main disadvantage with water stains is that they tend to raise the grain of the wood. A variety of measures can help minimize this effect. Working conditions can be a great help: wood

water stain you've just applied is to pre-soak and sand the wood first.

that has been acclimatized to an atmosphere of reasonable warmth and humidity is less thirsty than dry, cold wood. Wood that has been sanded really smooth with fine sandpaper has a tighter, less porous surface texture than rough, or roughly sanded wood. The tendency for the stain to dry streakily because of uneven absorption (although this can sometimes be a pretty effect in itself) can be helped either by giving the surface a coat of thin size or very thin shellac first. This tendency to patchiness does mean that water stains are best used on light, close-grained woods rather than on the porous, open-grained softwoods, where the paler, spring-grown areas will drink up the stain and the hard, autumn-grown grain remains almost impervious.

Spirit stains These hardly raise grain at all, but they are penetrative stains that dry very quickly, making it difficult to keep a wet edge going and avoid

patchiness. It is especially important not to cover the same area twice in a single application, or there will be some patches that are darker than others.

Oil stains These stains are by far the easiest to apply, and, because they dry more slowly, they are the most likely to give an even colour, which makes them particularly suitable for floors. The drying time does, however, have its own disadvantages: it can take as much as two days and it must be completely dry before you apply varnish.

❚ *Preparation* Stains are generally best applied to clean, untreated wood, with the exceptions mentioned above. Before staining, the surface should be scrubbed, sanded with fine sandpaper and rubbed over with a rag moistened in mineral spirits to cut any remaining

excess and even out the colour. Apply water and spirit stains quickly and methodically and do not cut corners, such as trying to avoid second or third coats by putting too much on at once. This will slow down the drying time and only encourage patchiness. Oil stains should be thinned and applied more liberally, especially on hard woods where you can risk leaving them to soak in for a few minutes before wiping off the surplus with a rag. Wiping off is something many people neglect, but it is this that actually makes the difference, on all staining, between a densely coloured surface where the grain is partially obscured and one where both grain and texture show attractively through the colour.

DECORATIVE STAINING

Although it is harder to contain stain than paint in specific chosen areas, there are several methods that will allow different colours, depths and patterns to be achieved on a single surface. You can make clear or coloured patterns on a stained ground by stencilling them in knotting or spirit varnish, tinting these if you want colour, and then using water stains, which will not affect the patterned areas. If a coat of clear size is put on to bare wood, patterns can be painted on top, and the size may then be washed off and then the surrounding surface stained. Outlining areas with fine dark lines of oil-based paint will keep different stain colours apart and is another way of making patterns. If you want the lines to show as natural wood through the stain, you will need to size the wood first and use a 'resist' of Brunswick black to paint the lines; let them dry, wash off the size, water-stain and then use a rag and plenty of mineral spirits to remove the lines.

Various areas of a wood surface can also be stained to different depths of colour using water stains and clear spirit varnish as the 'resist'; stain the

grease. Take care always to sand with the grain; cross-scratches will show in the finish and they will have to be removed with a scraper and the surface sanded again. When using water or spirit stains, fill deep scratches, scores or nail-holes before staining with one of the suitable proprietary fillers and touch up the filled and sanded areas with thin knotting to prevent them taking up more stain than the wood. Also remember that end grain will take up more stain so either apply the stain sparingly or wet the surface just before staining with mineral spirits. When using an oil stain, it's better to fill after staining with tinted wood filler.

■ *Method* A brush or rag-swab can be used to apply all the stains, and a clean rag should be kept handy to wipe off any

whole area with the lightest colour (or leave it bare if you want natural wood showing through), then varnish the areas you want to preserve in that colour. Stain with the next, deeper shade, then varnish again the parts you want to keep in that shade and continue with this sequence until your deepest stain colour has been applied. Then, either leave the varnished areas if you want a mildly embossed appearance, spirit-varnishing the whole surface, or remove the varnished areas with methylated spirits before applying one or more coats of polyurethane varnish.

BLEACHING

You may want to bleach wood, either to leave it in its natural, lighter state to apply a lighter-coloured stain than would show up on the original, or to give a faded look to a newly-stained surface. The traditional bleach materials for wood are oxalic acid and sodium hyposulphate (a concentrated version of domestic bleach and particularly good at removing red tones), bought from chemists and used separately or together. To use separately, dissolve 2oz (57g) of either crystal in 1¼ quarts (1.2 litres) of hot water and brush the solution on, when cool, with a fibre brush – you will ruin good bristle. For really good penetration, try sanding in the solution with fine wet-and-dry abrasive paper. When the surface is dry, brush off the crystals and neutralize it with a borax solution (one cup to one quart of water) or with methylated spirits, then wash off thoroughly with lots of vinegared water. (If anything, neutralize and wash off early rather than late to prevent the bleach drying in the grain, where it could affect both colour and quality of subsequent finishes. If the colour is not as pale as desired, you can always repeat the process.) If you use both solutions for a more thorough bleaching, use the oxalic acid first and let it half dry before applying the sodium hyposulphate, and try to do this in a well-ventilated area as the combination gives off powerful fumes.

To achieve a greyish tone on the wood, a weak to medium solution of permanganate helps kill yellow tones. Apply this before the neutralizing wash with borax solution, then follow the final washing stages as above. When really drastic bleaching is wanted, it is probably best to use the proprietary, two-pack alkaline-plus-peroxide bleaching system, available from builders' suppliers, although of course it is more costly. Any and all of these processes can be repeated until the desired shade is reached, but the washing off stages are vital. In the case of bleaching, there is no preventative measure against the inevitable raising of the grain, so be prepared for a considerable amount of sanding.

SPECIAL WOOD EFFECTS

Limed oak is oak which has been treated – or rather mistreated – in a way that turns it a distinctive grey-brown with white grain and pores. For a very pale version, bleach it first by one of the methods above before whitening the grain and pores. Otherwise, brush on a paste made of garden lime and water and leave it to dry before washing and sanding off the dry coating. (For a more pronounced effect, wire brush along the grain first to open it out.) Fill the grain and pores with plaster or proprietary filler, leave this to dry, then sand the

surface smooth and clean so that it remains in the cavities only. To avoid getting the slightest yellowy tinge back, finish with well-thinned white shellac rather than polyurethane varnish. Apply two or three coats, sanding between each coat and after the last one, as this finish is traditionally matt. For a slight sheen, polish with a white wax.

Weathered oak For this silver-grey look, do not fill the grain but simply treat the wood with lime, in this case allowing the sediment to settle before pouring off and using the solution. To preserve this delicate colouring, finish with white shellac as above.

Pickled pine looks like ordinary pine from which the paint has been stripped, leaving it both a more 'distressed' and paler version of its normal self. It is a shame to use this effect on a piece of well-grained pine with a good colour, but it can make nondescript pieces more interesting by intensifying the natural contrasts in the grain. The 'pickling' solution is made by adding one part nitric acid to eight parts water (don't mix the other way round); brush this evenly over the surface and let it dry. Sand down with very fine abrasive paper and, to kill any remaining yellowish tinges, brush over again with a mild solution of bichromate of potash. Rinse thoroughly when dry. Sand lightly again, if necessary, and protect with thinned white shellac as above or, for a more durable finish, with acid-catalyzed lacquer. For a slight sheen, polish the dry, lacquered surface with fine steel wool and wax; this should bring out a good colour.

It is extremely important to note that the materials used in bleaching and for the special wood effects can damage skin and other materials. Wear gloves, protective clothing and cover the surrounding area with suitable material.

GLAZING

In general terms, a glaze is any transparent or semi-transparent colour applied over another to enrich or intensify it, to subdue it, to 'age' it or to modify it in any other way. To narrow this field down slightly; the word 'glaze' tends to be used to indicate transparent colour of the oil-based type, which differentiates it from, for example, the water-based materials used for colour-washing. However, glaze is also sometimes called 'scumble' or 'scumble glaze' – especially in Britain – and the two should not be confused. Scumble can be oil- or water-based, but is always and only made from semi-transparent pigments, so that it has a degree of opacity. The ground coat therefore shows through to a much lesser and often random degree so that whether or not it is to be 'distressed' to produce a broken colour effect, it usually needs working on in some way, if only with a fine hair-stippler, to get even coverage. Don't try using scumble, therefore, when what you want is clear, translucent colour and don't confuse glaze with varnish, either; glaze is purely decorative, varnish is basically protective and although it's also used for various levels of shine and can itself be tinted, it cannot generally be worked on in the same way.

Oil-based glazes – which can be glossy, satin-finish or flat – are slicker, more sumptuous and more transparent than water-based washes. It is most likely that decorators first learned about their properties from artists who have traditionally used transparent colour to deepen shadows, enrich dark colour, highlight the lustre of silks, satins and the brilliance of jewels and give a pale translucency to skin tone, for glaze can do all this and more. In the decorator's craft, translucent colour on colour is used for atmosphere – for softness, richness and depth on surfaces, and to give a spacious feeling to walls and the patina of age to woodwork – as much as for the practical purpose of modifying an unsuccessful colour or the pure aesthetic pleasure of seeing colour through tone on translucent tone.

LEFT *A translucent glaze, tinted to tone with the ground, intensifies plain colour – even pastels – and gives them a depth of lustre which is more than either sheen or shine. In this room, the boarded ceiling is glazed to complement the walls, but with the tinted glaze applied brushily over a paler ground, then lightly and roughly dragged in the direction of the grain for surface texture.*

The effect of opaque colour is much easier to imagine than that of transparent colour. Opaque colour, in the form of paint, is what most of us are used to working with. It is not so much that glaze is more unpredictable, as paint can be full enough of surprises, but rather that it has an entirely different quality. If you're unfamiliar with glaze and the performance of transparent colour, it's especially useful to experiment on sealed or painted lining paper or board first, as you may find you want to change the tone of the ground colour as well as the glaze. As a general guide, you'll find that translucent glazes that are darker than the ground will add warmth; that a slightly lighter tone of a bright colour will add brilliance; that a glaze in a dark, cool colour over a warm ground will contribute richness and depth, and that a glaze which is very much lighter than a dark ground will give it a cooler tone.

■ *Preparation* The low-lustre, hard, nonporous surface of eggshell paint makes the ideal ground for all types of glaze as it provides some 'grip', but won't be softened or in any other way affected by it. Flat oil paint is the next best ground and although you can apply these glazes over emulsion, its porous finish makes the glaze harder to manipulate and achieve good, even results.

■ *Materials* *Oil glaze* You can buy ready-made glaze in a range of colours, but it is preferable to buy the clear variety and tint it yourself. Off-the-shelf, it comes in a variety of fairly thick consistencies; these can all be applied undiluted, as long as they're brushed out well. If you apply too thick a coat, it can form a surface skin which prevents the glaze beneath drying out properly and leaves it permanently soft. The level of sheen also varies according to the amount the glaze is thinned and you might well find the softer sheen of a well-thinned glaze much more attractive. You can thin glaze up to 1:2 with mineral spirits, but start with 1:1 mix and test before adding more solvent.

The more you add, the quicker the glaze will dry, which is obviously a disadvantage if you're planning to work on it with brushes, rags, combs and so on. If you want to slow the drying process, try thinning with one part raw linseed oil to two or three parts mineral spirits – this will only slightly increase the level of shine. If you want the glaze to dry more quickly, particularly when the weather is exceptionally damp or cold or you've tinted with one of the slower drying pigments, add just a little liquid drier; but watch the amount carefully or you could end up with the surface-skin problem mentioned above. The other problem with oil glazes is their limited availability. They tend to be stocked only by specialist or trade decorators' suppliers. You can make your own by mixing one part boiled linseed oil with between one and three parts pure turpentine. The glaze dries more quickly with a higher ratio of turpentine, so if you're using only the same amount of turpentine as oil, add an equal amount of drier and be

RIGHT *A daring treatment where two coats of blue-tinted glaze have been used to give depth to the surface of walls already colour-washed in dark-on-mid blue. Although, for walls, glaze can be a finishing coat in itself, these walls were varnished for additional sheen. But for any floor on which a glaze is used, like this marble 'tiled' version, varnish is a must – at least three coats for protection and durability.*

RIGHT *Glaze is here used more for texture than for sheen, or even colour, to add a light, dragged surface to these kitchen units. Part of the charm of this treatment is in the balance of plain and textured surfaces and although a definite method has been followed, the impression is actually of a random, refreshingly arbitrary choice of which bit to treat in what way.*

prepared for it still to take a week or more to dry out completely. Commercial glazes normally dry out overnight, although they'll take two or three days to harden off.

Paint glaze Neither of the two glazes mentioned here are completely transparent because they contain opaque pigment, but for this reason they have a softer effect and are both suitable for a variety of 'distressing' effects. The first type is a 1:1 mixture of flat oil paint or undercoat and oil glaze. Thinning the paint/glaze blend with an equal amount of mineral spirits makes a

very easily manipulated mixture that stays wet long enough to be worked on; adding more glaze will make it less opaque and help it hold out even longer. This glaze dries to a slight sheen, but gives a flatter finish than transparent oil glaze on its own.

For the flattest of paint glazes, simply use flat oil paint or undercoat well-thinned with mineral spirits. The disadvantage of this glaze is the speed with which it dries, but practice and, if you're distressing the glaze, having two people on the job, makes it an absolutely practical proposition. Many people

prefer the flat, almost sheenless finish. Thin the paint from 1:1 to 1:2 with solvent, starting with equal parts and testing before adding more solvent. If the glaze gets too runny to hold the effect you're working into it, simply add a little more paint or, if you don't want to increase the opacity, a little drier.

Varnish glaze This is simply tinted varnish – a useful way of giving woodwork, in particular, a clear coating that is both decorative and protective with an easily available material. Follow the instructions given for tinting, thinning and applying varnish, bearing in mind that adding colour will thicken the varnish so that it may need a little more solvent to thin it sufficiently to achieve a fine film of transparent colour. If you're tinting with any of the slower-drying pigments, you may need to add a spot or two of drier to speed the drying up.

Tinting glazes All of these glazes can be tinted with either universal stainers or the larger, better range of artists' oil colours. Dissolve the colours in a small amount of mineral spirits, stirring them

ABOVE *Different levels of sheen in a room play as much a part in textural variety as the more obvious rough and smooth, but varnish can get so stuck with its 'protective' image that its relative visual possibilities are forgotten. In this bedroom, the varnished surfaces are understated – nothing shines – and their relationship is unconventional: the furniture is satin-finished and the floor is actually matt, although over several coats of gloss varnish for durability.*

well until you have pure, thick liquid colour, containing no bits. (Some professionals insist on straining glazes to double-check for undissolved pigment which could streak the work surface.) To get proper colour dispersion, stir the unthinned glaze or paint into the colour a little at a time (not the other way around). In a paint/glaze mix, tint the paint rather than the glaze and for any of the paint glazes, buy white paint to make pale glazes but, for darker colour, buy the nearest you can get to your chosen tone and make the final tinting adjustment yourself.

▌ *Method* Glaze can be applied with either a brush or a rag. Over large areas, a brush is faster and makes it easier to control the amount of glaze you're

applying and achieve an even distribution. Brushing technique is much the same as for normal painting. Use a 3 or 4in (7.5 or 10cm) brush so that you can apply the glaze as quickly as possible. Pick up a small amount of glaze at a time, brush it on and smooth it out quickly to a thin film with the brush tip to avoid runs. If you're using a rag, bunch it up in your hand, dip it into the glaze and simply wipe it on thinly over the surface. If you're planning to use more than one layer of transparent/semi-transparent colour, let each coat dry out overnight before applying the next. Whether or not you intend to distress the glaze for a broken colour finish, you can even out patchy colour with a hair-stripper, which is an attractive finish in itself. Remember, too, that glaze is a decorative, but not a protective finish. If you want proper protection for your hard-won decoration, it's only sensible to give it one or more coats of clear varnish.

VARNISHING

Varnish is almost as large and complex an area as paint. There are innumerable specialist products, most of which you don't need to know about, but there are two or three which between them give the adequate variety of finishes normally needed and wanted in interior work. The choice between them is not only a matter of practicality but aesthetics. Each finish has a different quality as well as a different performance and is used as much to visually enhance the surface beneath as to protect it.

Polyurethane varnish This is the modern, jack-of-all-trades among varnishes. It is the easiest one to use, the most economical and the most versatile, in that it is applicable to practically all interior surfaces, except plastics and those that may contain alkaline residue from insufficiently neutralized treatments such as stippling with caustic soda. As a finish, polyurethane doesn't perhaps have the subtlety of some of the traditional varnishes, although if you are prepared to work patiently with it, laying on thin coats one after another, and playing around with the various degrees of sheen available, you can achieve a high quality finish, which is unbeatable for surface protection and durability. Polyurethane varnish comes in clear, wood and some coloured finishes; you can also tint it yourself by dissolving artists' oil colour in mineral spirits and adding varnish to it, a little at a time and stirring well. Today's clear polyurethanes are virtually colourless. The palest – and you need to check that is what you are getting – have only a very slightly yellowish tone which make them suitable for covering all but the most precisely and delicately coloured surfaces. To compensate for the yellowish tinge either modify the colour beneath it or the varnish itself with a small amount of cobalt blue oil paint or artists' oil colour, but you may prefer to use a 'water-white' protective finish, such as shellac, mentioned below.

Polyurethane varnish is normally obtainable in three finishes: matt, which has almost no sheen at all, satin, which has a sheen similar to that of eggshell paint, and gloss, which is just what it says – a hard, high shine. The level of shine goes hand-in-hand with durability, gloss being the most durable. However, you may not want a high-gloss finish, not least because it demands a near-perfect surface as it shows up every imperfection and speck of dust or grit. In this case, the way to achieve a high level of protection and durability and a low level of sheen is to build up the surface with two or more coats of gloss and finish with a satin coat – or even a matt coat, although it will take a couple of coats of matt over gloss to achieve an even finish.

Varnish is like paint in that several thinned coats make a smoother, more even and glass-like surface than a couple of thick ones. The only exception is in varnishing floors when two

LEFT AND ABOVE *Hiding under many a peeling, painted surface is good wood and this, of course, applies as much to furniture as to interior woodwork. The transformation that can be achieved with thorough stripping, meticulous sanding and several careful coats of varnish is little short of miraculous.*

undiluted coats should be applied after a well-diluted sealing coat (up to half and half with the appropriate solvent), to set up a really durable base. The 'proper' tool for applying varnish is an oval varnish brush, specially made to hold more varnish than an ordinary brush and so improve its flow; but, as with other finishes, there are alternatives. A 2 or 3in (5 or 7cm) paintbrush will do perfectly well, with the addition of a smaller artists' brush – 1 or ½in (2.5 or 1.2cm) – for detail work. Whatever you use, keep the brush exclusively for varnish work; clean brushes in mineral spirits and twirl them dry. Shaking varnish can cause it to froth and the same thing happens if you shake the brush – both could create bubbles on the varnish surface.

Polyurethane varnishes are normally touch-dry in a couple of hours and can be recoated in five to six hours. The next coat should be applied as soon as possible after this, as it is less likely to adhere properly once the varnish is completely dry. In traditional varnish work, 'flatting down' between coats is an integral part of the process, but polyurethanes are less elastic than some of the older types of varnish and therefore need to be rubbed down and polished with care. Matt varnish does not really need rubbing down between coats; the first coat of a satin and gloss varnish should definitely not be rubbed down and preferably not the second either, or there is a risk of breaking through the fine film to the surface beneath. Observe the recoating time strictly, as this will help adhesion, and on subsequent coats, use fine abrasive paper or steel wool.

■ *Preparation* It is worth being meticulous about preparation for varnish work. Varnishing works best in a clean, warm, dry environment. Clean, sweep and vacuum the room you're working in, preferably without raising dust as you do so (wet sawdust helps keep dust down) and shut off the room until the varnish is dry. Professionals go

to exaggerated lengths to prepare and protect varnish: allowing it to warm to room temperature, like wine, to improve its 'flow'; using absolutely clean cans and giving the inside of any clean but previously used can a coat of knotting to seal any loose particles; using one can inside another so that the brush may be scraped against the outer can without risk of contaminating the varnish with dust, grit or loose hairs; straining varnish into the inner can through muslin to avoid lumps; making quite sure of a dust-free surface by wiping it with a tack rag before varnishing; preparing brushes by working them into a little spare varnish first and pouring only a little varnish into the inner can at a time, so that it can be thrown away without waste if anything contaminates it. How far you choose to follow their example will depend on patience and perfectionism, but if you want a good finish, it is worth taking the trouble to

make sure that you achieve it; otherwise there really is little point in trying the technique as it will not live up to your expectations as it should.

■ *Method* When varnishing *walls*, thin satin or gloss varnish 3:1 with mineral spirits – it will run on more easily and leave a smoother finish. Dip the brush into the varnish to about half-bristle length and then transfer it straight to the surface. The feel of brush against wall – whether it drags, or slips too easily – will indicate whether the loading is right. If you have overloaded the brush, press the bristles against the inside of the can to release the surplus, but do not tip off the excess on the top edge of the can or you will risk getting bubbles. Applying the varnish generously will help to give an even coverage. Dip the brush in three or four times and cover the first section quickly with easy, decisive but light strokes, to avoid creating bubbles, and pick or flick

out any foreign bodies with the tip of the brush. Leave this section to settle for as long as it takes you to brush on the next and then, with an empty brush (scraping it off on the outer can, if you're using one, otherwise on clean paper), return to the first section, crossing your brush strokes to lay the varnish in and finishing with a light, upward stroke. To avoid getting beads of varnish on areas such as picture rails, the top inch or so can be finished horizontally.

The same general principles apply to varnishing *woodwork*, but there are a few specific precautions and procedures worth knowing. Varnish does not adhere well to a greasy surface and may even start to 'ciss' in places. Bare surfaces

can develop their own form of greasiness in a matter of days so, if there is any doubt, give the surface a wet-rub with either vinegared-water and wet-and-dry abrasive paper, a chamois leather and water mixed with a little whiting or a rag moistened with mineral spirits. Try to avoid touching the surface subsequently – fingers contain a surprising amount of grease. If you are varnishing all the woodwork in a room, follow the normal painting sequence doing doors first, and ending on skirting boards this is a fail-safe method for making sure the brush is worked in and clean by the time you reach the largest, and most obvious flat surface, skirting boards being the area where you are most likely to pick up dust again.

Doors should be taken off their hinges where possible, working on the flat allows the varnish to 'flow' over the surface rather than being simply brushed on. Work with a full brush on horizontal surfaces from the middle of each section, easing the varnish out to the edges, before actually brushing it out lightly and evenly over the whole area and laying it off in the direction of the grain. How many coats to apply is simply a matter of patience – or rather, lack of it – versus perfectionism, but the greater the number of well-laid, thinned coats of varnish, the better protected and more mirror-like the surface. Matt varnish should need no more than three coats, but satin can take up to five and gloss up to seven. However many coats you use, the proper, professional way is to lay off alternate coats against, and finishing coats with, the grain.

One of the big advantages of polyurethane varnish is that it does give a reasonable finish with a brush, unlike many of the traditional ones which need to be applied with a rubber. Nevertheless, however careful you are brush strokes may still show on the finished work. For a soft, smooth sheen, sand the last coat when dry with very fine abrasive paper and then with very fine steel wool and liquid wax, both with the grain. For a brilliant polish, wet-rub along the grain with very fine, wet-and-dry abrasive paper and wash off any residue with clean water. When the surface is dry, make a 'rubber' out of lint-free cotton wrapped around a pad of cotton batting; moisten the pad with oil (warmed linseed oil is ideal, although lemon, olive or baby oil will do), pick up a little rotten-stone on the pad from a saucer and rub this in a circular movement over the surface. Don't rub too vigorously or too long in the same place or you may heat and soften the varnish with the friction. The final stage is to wipe the surface clean and then rub it with dry household flour, using either a soft cloth or the palm of your hand.

Polyurethane varnish can be applied over any well-seasoned, well-established and sanded wood *floor*. Because the aim is to build up an exceptionally well-bonded, durable surface, varnishing is treated a little differently on floors. It is worth applying a sealing coat first; diluting the varnish half and half with mineral spirits. The first couple of coats are then applied undiluted, brushed on against the grain, and laid off with it. Subsequent coats can be thinned and applied with a rubber, if you wish, but leave each coat to dry overnight and sand down before applying the next, vacuuming thoroughly and preferably using a tack rag to make sure the surface is spotless. The number of coats is a matter of personal preference,

although three is the absolute minimum, and five or six are advisable on a floor that receives much wear and tear. This applies whichever type of varnish you are using. The prime aim with floors is protection and gloss varnish, although the slowest drying is by far the most durable. The high shine will dull with wear, but if you prefer not to have it from the start, either finish with a satin coat or wait until the least coat is really dry and hard (this will take up to a week), then rub it along the grain first with medium, then fine steel wool.

LACQUER

Strictly speaking, none of the finishes below can be called 'lacquer', since the original, fine oriental lacquer-work depended on the sap of the lac tree and the patience of saint-like craftsmen, prepared to coat, rub down and polish a surface several dozen times. The result was a finish as smooth as satin and as hard as glass which, however brilliant or sombre the colour, created the illusion that you were looking into or through rather than at it. No techniques we have devised in the West, despite the efforts of skilled craftsmen to simulate the work of their Eastern counterparts with paint and shellac, quite match the wonderful ambiguity of this oriental finish, which is simultaneously hard and soft, brilliant and subtle. However, it is questionable whether it is even sensible to attempt this level of finish on most interior surfaces, especially those subject to wear and tear like doors. Hard as it is, it is not invulnerable to chipping and the slightest damage shows up painfully on such a high sheen surface and can make it look shabby in a trice. Lacquer-type finishes make heavy demands on preparation for the same reason. Walls and woodwork must be absolutely smooth and even and it's better to confine a high-gloss finish on walls to rooms with good, plain proportions, as light bouncing in all directions off different angles,

RIGHT *Another inspirational piece of lacquer-work designed by Leon and Maurice Jallot in the late 1920s, as was the cabinet (below). For smaller pieces of areas of 'lacquer', like this little table, you may find the sheen of shellac more sympathetic than, say, satin-finish varnish.*

ABOVE *Traditional lacquer-work has a quality of shine which no other finish can approach and the point is made very clearly here in the visible difference between the hard-soft depth of sheen on the surface of the lacquer cabinet and the more brittle, superficial shine on the varnished wall behind.*

extrusions and alcoves will confuse and disturb rather than please and satisfy the eye. Yet all this is said to be cautionary rather than off-putting, as there are a variety of fairly simple ways to produce something like a lacquer finish, modern varnishes to protect them and the results are far from the thick texture and hard shine of a coat of gloss paint. The secret lies in the number of coats of clear or tinted glaze and varnish you have the patience to apply, for every extra coat will add to the depth and subtlety of the surface.

WALLS

Since the instruction for surface preparation as well as mixing and applying the various materials are detailed elsewhere in the relevant sections of this book, all that needs to be said here is which blend of materials will give you which type of finish.
If you are satisfied with the colouring of the walls and merely want to give them sheen or shine, a couple of coats of satin or gloss varnish will do the trick. But by tinting the varnish you can modify the base colour: adding a small amount of colour that tones with the ground to gloss varnish can give it a jewel-like intensity, while adding a small amount of one of the more earthy colours to satin-finish varnish can have a softening and ageing effect. To build up a surface which has both depth of colour and shine, apply a number of coats of tinted glaze, modifying each coat through different tones of the ground colour before you finish with clear or tinted varnish.

WOODWORK

Despite the *caveats*, 'lacquering' can completely transform the most nondescript piece of wood and is therefore particularly suitable for those plain, ordinary, very modern flush doors. But preparation is all. Unless wood has a sufficiently fine grain and smooth surface to need undercoat only, be prepared to fill, sand and prime until it is really hard and completely flat. Use wood filler or all-purpose proprietary filler to correct any major, obvious gouges, chips, scores or other defects, then mix the all-purpose filler to the consistency of cream and brush it on like paint, first across and then with the grain; a sponge can also be useful for filling door sides. On brand new flush doors – especially those made of foreign ply – you may have not only grain to contend with, but a kind of 'furry' texture which will persist through the first filling/sanding at least; but once you've primed it, then filled, sanded and primed again, it should disappear. Keep following the fill/sand/prime sequence until you have as near a glass-like, hard smoothness as possible, then give the surface a couple of well-thinned undercoats before painting.

More expensive, but with a china-glaze quality of finish to match is synthetic gesso, available from artists' suppliers. This is the stuff artists use to prime canvases and in decorating it will provide a smooth, hard shell even over previously painted surfaces, as long as they're well sanded first to give them tooth. With synthetic gesso, you can leave out the priming stage of the raw-wood process above, brushing on thin coat after thin coat, leaving each to dry before sanding well with medium abrasive paper or steel wool and dusting off between coats. Seal the last coat with well-thinned shellac before painting. Whether you're using proprietary, all-purpose filler or gesso, use old brushes that you will never again need to use for paint. Don't skimp on the sanding – as with paint, it's the many fine layers which will build up to a good, hard, smooth surface – and sand especially well along the closing edges of doors or windows, even to the point where the old finish just shows through or they may not shut properly.

The method for achieving a 'lacquered' wood surface relies on paint and varnish and/or glaze in much the same way as it does for walls. The ground-work is important: apply two or three thinned coats of flat oil-based paint or undercoat, rubbing down between coats with fine, wet-and-dry abrasive paper and soapy water. Rinse off thoroughly each time, allow the surface to dry and go over it with a tack rag. Then apply two or three coats of gloss or satin polyurethane varnish, thinned 3:2 with mineral spirits, rubbing down between coats as above. As with 'lacquered' walls, tinted glaze and varnish coats will give greater depth of colour. Polish the last varnish coat either with oil and rotten-stone or, for a higher shine, with wax.

SHELLAC

Shellac is probably best known as the material used for French polishing for which, to quell both hopes and fears immediately, this book does not to give the instructions. These are as complicated and patience-stretching as the method itself which, although it does result in a sheen of a particularly beautiful character, is a highly-skilled operation, not adequately taught by book and also more suitable to fine, old pieces of furniture than structural or decorative interior surfaces. Shellac is also not particularly durable; imaginative use of modern varnishes will not only give a very close approximation of its finish but a much better level of protection. However, this does not entirely rule out shellac as a finishing coat. Listed below are a few methods for those who want to use it as such. It can also play other very practical roles in the decorating process.

Liquid shellac is a spirit varnish made from an insect-derived resin dissolved in methylated spirits. Since it is soluble only in methylated spirits (and, therefore, alcohol) it makes an extremely useful barrier coat between different stages of decoration,

ABOVE *Probably the nearest we get to a lacquer finish today is by having a surface commercially sprayed with one of the modern artificial versions, such as nitro-cellulose lacquer, and this really does need to be done professionally. But the level of finish achievable by hand should still not be dismissed, if you're prepared to lay on several coats of glaze – up to a dozen.*

preventing one layer 'disturbing' another with unwanted chemical reactions and allowing mistakes to be cleaned off without damage to the ground. Its fast drying time – about one hour for each coat, but increasingly faster the more its thinned – which is precisely what makes French polishing so tricky, is one of its main advantages in other applications. Its sealing properties are also often used in the preparatory stages of decorating: the best knotting, which prevents resinous knots and streaks in wood from 'bleeding' into subsequent finishes, is pure shellac, and it will also seal off new plaster patches, plaster board before papering and filler before painting, the only proviso being that its glossy surface has insufficient key for oil-based primers and should therefore be sanded with medium abrasive paper or touched up with sharp flat paint first ('sharp' means very well thinned with mineral spirits). Shellac is also used as a kind of 'invisible mend' filler on unpainted wood: flowed in liquid shellac can fill minor depressions caused by over zealous sanding and, in its solid form of shellac sticks, which come in various colours, can be melted with a hot iron into cracks or areas of exceptionally open grain.

■ *Buying and using* Shellac in varnish form comes in a variety of colours including the orange-yellow type known as 'button polish', a brown sometimes called 'garnet', a light amber known as 'pale', a milky white and a near-transparent water-white; solutions of Bismark brown are sometimes added to give it a reddish colour, spirit black for black polish and you can tint shellac yourself with spirit-soluble dyes. The most useful of the commercial varieties is the water-white, as it has just about the least self-colour of any clear finish available. It has a shelf life of about six months maximum and after that may not dry properly, or at all. It's therefore worth getting it from a well-patronized, specialist shop, looking for a date on the tin and even asking if you can test it on a piece of wood. For most purposes, thin shellac from 2:1 to 1:1 with methylated spirit, several thin coats being better than one thick one. Ignore the manufacturer's instructions to shake the tin before opening it: shellac should always be stirred, not shaken, otherwise you'll cause bubbles which will show up on the surface of the work. It's also important to use shellac in warm, dry conditions – a damp atmosphere may cause a white bloom in the finish – and to observe the same dust-eliminating precautions as for varnish. And as with varnish, keep one brush especially for shellac: a soft-bristled 1½ or 2in (3.8 or 5cm) brush is best, cleaned with

methylated spirits after use. Soften hard brushes in a mild solution of ammonia, but never use soap.

■ *Method* *Brushing on* The most important aspect of brushing shellac on is that you work as quickly and methodically as possible. Shellac begins to dry almost before the brush has finished each stroke, leaving you no opportunity to fill in missed bits or overlap wet edges – at least until the next coat when you may, anyway, start to get a patchy build up of film. Practise applying shellac on a spare piece of wood until you can apply it quickly, evenly and confidently, without panic. It also helps if you can work on a flat surface so, for example, take doors off hinges first.

Take up a full brush-load each time, pressing any excess out against the inside of the can to avoid bubbles, rather than across the rim. Place the tip of the brush in the centre of the surface and, working with the grain, draw it lightly across to one edge; then go back to the centre and draw the brush out to the opposite edge in the same way. If you've loaded the brush correctly, there should be enough varnish left in the small, central pool to repeat this stage once, before, pressing slightly harder on the brush, you level this area out by brushing right across the surface from edge to edge. Take care not to stop short of the edge – imagine the brush is a plane landing and taking off, so that the movement of the brush begins and ends well clear of each edge. Try not to overlap brush strokes and re-load the brush quickly as and when necessary, repeating the whole process above each time. Rub down between coats with very fine abrasive paper or fine steel wool, dusting off residue with a dry cloth and tack rag. Use steel wool and soapy water to even out any patches on the dry surface, or use a rag moistened with methylated spirits, which softens the shellac and allows it to flow together.

If the shellac is intended to be a final coat, you may want to eliminate some of

its shine. Wait until the surface is completely dry and hard, then sprinkle on a little flour-fine pumice powder and, with a soft-bristled brush such as a shoebrush, work backwards and forwards over the whole surface, from edge to edge with one stroke and staying absolutely true to the grain. This will give you a fine, matt finish with no criss-crossing effect. On dark woods, mixing charcoal dust with the pumice will stop any powder stuck in cracks from showing up. You can also use felt or a soft rag, moistened with a mixture of baby oil and mineral spirits and sprinkled with pumice for this process, which will leave you with a fine, dulled, satin-smooth, satin sheen.

Rubbing on In French polishing proper, the shellac is traditionally applied with a rubber – a piece of fine, soft, lint-free cloth, such as old sheeting, wrapped around a wad of cotton batting (which acts as a reservoir for the polish) to form a pad. There is an easier approximation to this process for clear-finishing wood that is sometimes called 'dip and rub' and which produces a finish with a rich, soft gloss. First brush on a 1:2 mix of shellac and pure turpentine, leave this to dry and then sand down with fine abrasive paper or steel wool. Make up the 'rubber' as described above and dip it first into a saucer or small bowl of turpentine, then one of shellac and rub it on to the wood with circular or figure-of-eight movements. In this process you will inevitably be overlapping strokes, but try to work your way across the surface methodically, don't go back over areas you've left and above all, keep the rubber moving continuously until the whole surface is evenly covered. Let the first coat dry for three to four hours, then repeat the process at least three times to make quite sure that you have a well covered and, also, an even, smooth finish for the most satisfactory result. It really is worth taking the trouble with this number of coats, to achieve the desired effect and one which will last.

DECORATIVE DETAIL

LINING

This is one of the simplest ways to add interest to plain surfaces and emphasize or visually alter their proportions. A series of lines can be painted on to an expanse of wall, to break the area up into panels. The placing and scale of the lines can be used to make the wall seem taller or shorter, wider or narrower, or to contain areas of, say, broken colour, marbling or tortoiseshell. On woodwork, lining can be used to transform a set of nondescript flush doors into prettily panelled pieces, or simply as decoration – a fine line along each side of a balustrade or around the top edge of a mantelpiece. It can also be used to emphasize the straight and curved relief on mouldings in either wood or plaster.

The choice of colour for lining is an individual matter, but as a general principle, it should either tone with the ground – on plain walls, for example, the same colour but a shade or two deeper – or at least be sympathetic to some other element in the decoration: on tortoiseshell panels where the deepest and most dominant colour is dark brown, this would also be the most suitable choice for a fine, containing line.

■ ***Materials*** The lining colour needs to be fairly thin to flow, although obviously where lining a light colour over dark, it must be substantial enough to cover the ground. Dissolve artists' oil colour or universal stainer in a small amount of mineral spirits and mix this solution with a little varnish, or quicker-drying goldsize, to give it 'body' and hold the bristles of the brush together for a clean edge. Thin with mineral spirits, and if the mixture doesn't flow quite smoothly enough, add just a drop or two of raw linseed oil. Perfectionists will also strain the colour before use to be sure there are no particles of undissolved pigment, or anything else.

The professional's tools for lining are especially made, hog-hair fitches, round or flat for different purposes; the short-haired fitches are easier to use for the beginner, but the long-haired ones hold more paint so you don't have to pick up colour as often. Artists' sable brushes are a perfectly satisfactory alternative for the amateur and two sizes should provide sufficient versatility, a No 6 for broader lines, ⅛–½in (3–12mm), and a No 3 for lines of ¹⁄₁₆in (1.5mm) or less.

■ *Method* Lining can often frighten people because it seems to demand artistic ability and, above all, a steady hand. The first thing to remember is that you are not being asked to do a technical drawing – decoration is a handicraft, not a mechanical skill, and the evidence of the hand of the craftsmen is part of the charm. Second, it is easy enough to practise on painted board or lining paper. Third, there are both preventative and curative measures for imperfect lines. A coat of clear varnish before lining will enable you to wipe off mistakes before they dry with a rag moistened in mineral spirits. On other surfaces, keep paper tissues handy to wipe off the worst of any slips; when the paint is dry, rub out the mistakes with fine abrasive paper, steel wool or a pencil eraser. Try to avoid rubbing through into the base coat, because although you can retouch lines – lightly to avoid colour variation – retouching the ground will almost certainly show, as paint starts to fade in a matter of days. If it is necessary to retouch the base coat, gently feather the patch into the surrounding area, either with a very fine abrasive or with your finger.

There are a variety of tricks to ensure a true line, straight or curved. For short, straight lines, turning the bevelled side of a ruler to the wall will keep its edge clear; some decorators glue corks to the underside of longer straight-edges to hold them off the wall, and maintain a steady hand by resting the middle finger on the straight-edge as the brush is drawn down or across the wall. Snapped, ruled or freehand chalk lines are an ideal way not only to guide hand and eye when it comes to painting in the lines, but to judge initially whether they are in the right position and quantity. Be sure not to leave too much chalk on the surface; lightly dust off any loose surplus before you paint, or it could clog the brush. Whatever method you use, wipe the painting edge regularly to minimize the risk of blobs. When lining

FAR LEFT *The unusual ceiling detail in this room has been picked out in electric blue, echoing the neon lighting.*

ABOVE LEFT *Skilfully done, outlining panels in darker colours can emphasize (or create) a sense of three-dimensions as demonstrated here in these kitchen units.*

ABOVE *The cool elegance of classical detailing is brought out in this treatement of the panels, doorcase and architrave of this entrance. Choosing the right toning shades is just as important as skill in execution.*

an edge freehand, especially curves on woodwork, use a notched card as a guide for placing little dots of paint every few inches to mark the position of the line. When it comes to painting the line, rest your little finger against the edge of the piece you are working on to steady your hand. To keep both hands free for this sort of work, some painters carry the colour in a mug, strapped through the handle and around the waist.

All precautions and remedies apart, sooner or later the time comes when you've actually got to paint that first line. Pick up enough colour on the brush so that it's well but not overloaded, or it may produce a blob (press the brush gently against the inside of your paint pot to release excess colour). For a long, single stroke, hold the brush as far up the handle as possible while still feeling comfortable with it. Stand far enough away from the painting surface for extended arm and brush to reach it easily and, keeping your arm relaxed –

let your shoulder muscles do the work as you literally draw the line. A little practice doing it this way and then using wrist, elbow and so on will demonstrate how much easier it is with this method to get a free, steady and continuous line. Once the brush is on the surface, keep going – even if the start is wobbly – because any hesitation or stopping and starting will show. Another trick is not to look at the brush, but to keep looking ahead to where you want it to go; trust the hand to follow the eye and it will. The amount of pressure, rather than the brush itself, will determine the width of the stripe, so keep pressure even for an even stripe and, for fine lines, use only the tip.

Once you become confident with the technique, a variety of effects can be tried. Using water-thin paint can produce lines that look faded with age. This effect can also be achieved by using thicker paint and, when it's dry, sanding it.

ABOVE *An original use of moulding – with recesses picked out in gold but the top, curved edges left to stand out in white – changes not only the dimensions but the entire status of this ordinary flush door. Grilled cupboard doors concealing radiators are given the same treatment.*

FAKE PANELLING

This is an extension of lining, but, in this case, you really are trying to deceive the eye rather than just create an honest decorative effect. As with lining, this *trompe l'oeil* technique can be used on walls, to add interest to a set of plain flush doors or to any woodwork surface – for example, the panel that typically fills in the triangular area between stairs and floor in a hall. For this job, use paint to match the ground, tinted with either artists' oil colours/universal stainers for oil-based paint or, for water-based paint, with universal stainers or artists' gouache, acrylic or powder colours. You will also need a ½in (1.2cm) brush with

a square end (either a proper decorators' fitch or an artists' brush), a straight-edge, chalk or a sharp pencil, and masking tape if there is any doubt about your freehand painting abilities. When you have decided what kind of panels you want and where, mark their position with the straight-edge and pencil or chalk. Each panel requires a rectangle of parallel lines, ½in (1.2cm) apart and with 'mitred' corners. Tint the paint to give two shades, one just a little darker than the ground colour and one about the same amount darker again. The aim is to create an effect of light and shadow, so on each panel, use the light shade to fill in the tracks on the bottom and the side away from the main light source, and use the darker shade to fill in the others, making sure the shades meet neatly – use masking tape if necessary – at the 'mitred' corners.

This technique for creating light and shade is enormously versatile and can obviously be extended. You might, for example, want to create a very elaborate

ABOVE *As a general principle, the high relief work on mouldings is best left in a lighter colour, which follows the natural effects of light and shade. But the heaviest strip of moulding here would have stood out in too great a contrast had it been painted white, so the normal distribution of light and dark is reversed to integrate it with the other detail-work around it.*

RIGHT *The standpoint of the observer is often crucial to* trompe l'oeil*. The dramatic perspective of arches drawn on a wall is made more credible by the size of the building. The painted horizon is a trifle high, because if the observer could look down on it, it would not work.*

effect on 'panelled' doors and give them a dragged or grained finish. On walls, the panels could contain areas of a paint finish that differ from the ground. They could suggest a window where none exists, either by filling in the panels with mirror or by painting panes of blue sky, sponged with scudding, stylized grey and white clouds. Alternatively, the scale of the painting could be enlarged to suggest a deeper recess.

TROMPE L'OEIL

Trompe l'oeil is the technique of creating visual illusion. The earliest celebration of it is Pliny's well-known story from the fifth century BC of the good-natured contest between the painters Zeuxis and Parrhasios. Zeuxis painted a picture of grapes so well that birds flew up to peck them, then, seeing the curtain covering his colleague's picture, he asked for it to be drawn back. Parrhasios replied that the curtain was the picture, Zeuxis immediately ceded the prize to him, for he had succeeded in deceiving not only the birds, but also Zeuxis, an artist himself. Of course, the story is apocryphal and to judge visual art merely on its capacity to simulate three-dimensional space is naive; indeed, many cultures, particularly those of China and Japan,

have long held such things to be aesthetically childish; but as far as decorative painting is concerned, *trompe l'oeil* is a skill of the highest order. In fact, it would be wrong to infer that the amateur can produce such effects with ease; many are beyond the skill of all but a small number of artists. Nonetheless, it is surprising how much can be achieved by the lay person through a variation of the technique of lining, especially when it is augmented by some of the techniques previously described in this book.

The raised mouldings of doors, skirting boards and inset panels can all be simulated on a flat surface. Recesses

can be conjured up in the same manner, and an illusion of texture and space created where otherwise there might be only a bland, flat surface. These effects involve very simple manipulations of light and shade, using just two tones of colour closely related to the base colour of the surface.

▌*Materials* Most paint is suitable for this process. You can use artists' oils, diluted with mineral spirits; artists' acrylics, diluted with water and, if necessary, mixed with their own gel retarder; flat-oil, eggshell or undercoat tinted with artists' oils or universal stainers; or latex tinted with gouache, acrylics, stainers or powder colours. Generally speaking, you need the same brushes as for basic lining – a ½in (1.2cm) flat-ended one being the most useful general size – a straight-edge, chalk or a sharp pencil, and masking tape.

▌*Application* The basic technique is the same, however complex the ultimate effect may be. The elaboration is really dependent on one's own imagination,

and you may wish to copy a series of panel mouldings or carved surfaces. Even if you decide to copy a Rococo scroll by tracing the design and squaring it up, the lines you paint will be dictated by the effects of light and shadow around the outline of the three-dimensional form. The safest approach is to err on the side of simplicity.

When you have decided on the design, mark out its position with chalk or pencil and, if it consists mainly of straight edges, use a straight-edge to draw it. If you are evoking geometric raised mouldings surrounding panels, each panel will require a rectangle of parallel lines about ½in (1.2cm) apart, with mitred corners. Tint your paint to give two shades, one just a little bit

darker than the ground colour, the other darker again by the same proportion. Now decide where your light source is positioned – to the left or right. A simple track moulding should be shaded as follows: if the light is striking from the left, you shade the right side of the right-hand track lightly, and the left side of the left-hand track darkly. This gives the effect of a highlight striking on the left side because of the greater contrast there. If you wish to keep the tracks straight, use masking tape to make the mitre joint sharp. Set the tape at 45° to the rectangle and paint right up to it on one side with the appropriate tone for the area, then remove the tape. When that tone is dry, reapply the tape at the same angle but so that you can paint up

ABOVE *Another example of the difficulties of lighting trompe l'oeil. Had the angles of the walls been made into painted seaside awning poles and the ceiling corners into a beach-house eave and the awning, the illusion would be more credible. As it is, it's only partly successful.*

to the 45° join from the other side, with the other tone. The tape should shield the tone you've just done. This technique of creating light and shade can be taken to any degree of elaboration by careful repetition. it can be applied around or over rag-rolled, stippled, spattered and broken colour areas; over or around marbling, and around tortoiseshell and dragged areas, but not usually over them.

If you want to give the impression of a deep recess, say a rectangular one, lay in the shape of the implied rectangular moulding and then, on the inside of the inner line of one of the sides, extend the darker of the two shades inward for about a third of the way. Then draw a vertical to terminate it from top to bottom of the rectangle and stop the shade at this line. Next, at the lower corner of the side you've shaded from, extend a line upward diagonally toward the centre of the panel and, where it crosses the vertical you have just drawn, draw a horizontal line across to the opposite inner side of the panel. Then fill in this area with a slightly lighter shade of the ground colour.

Within the area of these painted panels you can add anything you wish. They are particularly useful for inserting mirrors, an area of differing texture to the rest of the decor – such as porphyry amid marbling – or even paintings. Stencils also fit well in them, and so does graining.

1

4

2

5

STENCILLING

Stencilling, like marbling and wood graining, is a technique that dates from antiquity. There are examples of it on surfaces from walls to shields, domestic houses to painted tombs. Its simplicity is equalled by its charm, and, on occasion, by its beauty, because it can be applied with great delicacy as well as with the more familiar bold effect. It can also be executed on almost any painted surface – provided that it is clean and sound – and many unpainted ones, including

3

6

LEFT AND RIGHT
Stencilling sequence
1 Fix the stencil-board firmly to the surface to be painted.
2 Apply paint vertically with a flat-ended stencil brush, using a pouncing action.
3 Press the stencil-board flat if necessary to stop paint getting under the edges.
4 When the first stage of the pattern is dry, apply the next.

5 Lift the stencils vertically, peeling backward, never sideways.
6 A basic shape carefully aligned on a grid can alternate various orders of a pattern.
7 This pattern can be touched up using an artists' brush or sign writers' 'pencil'.
8 This basic stencil can be used in a series of variations.

7

8

wood and metal. Its popularity has waned in Europe until recent years, due largely to the use of wallpapers and, in part, to its rather vulgar and heavy-handed use in the late Victorian period in England where it was often misapplied in a banal, grandiose manner without the delicacy and fineness of earlier periods.

In Europe, stencilling has tended to be more of an industrial process for much of this century, appearing on signs, aircraft and roads rather than in domestic interiors; sculptors have used it to the full on painted structures for its strength and crispness, but interior designers have only recently warmed to it, largely inspired by the work of one particular individual, Lyn Le Grice.

In America, it was better used from the start, and, indeed, the technique was largely preserved by American settlers who turned it to unpretentious good use as a form of decoration on plaster, floors and furniture in clapboard houses. As a result, it achieved status and has become part of American folk-art and culture.

On pale walls, either in a frieze pattern or as a pattern distributed from the corners spreading outward into the room, there is no real colour limitation, provided that the colours do not become too various and loud or the pattern confused and disjointed. Very muted colour can be particularly beautiful – on off-white walls, grey or blue-grey and beige patterning can make the wall look like a big, damasked cloth; or with a simple pattern of strong regularity you can use colour of almost Etruscan intensity – such as vibrant Indian red or deep, vivid blue. On woodwork, if it is clear and sealed, patterning of muted, warm earth colours and olives looks very well, giving that variety within unity that one sees in high quality marquetry. Woodwork that is painted overall can take areas of very intense colour; provided that it's not overdone, it can be extremely effective.

RIGHT *Subtle and graceful stencilling, applicable to many interiors, adds quiet panache to an upright piano.*

BELOW RIGHT *An elaborate stencil on a floor surface, abutting marble. A somewhat eccentric mixture but the colouring is well-balanced.*

As with most other decorative effects, it is always better to err on the side of restraint in stencilling; you can always strengthen what you've done, but it's very hard work toning it all down again, let alone taking out whole sections of a design. Strong patterning works well on floors, where you can 'paint your own rug' if you wish; you can, in fact, use stencilling anywhere in any room – provided that you protect it with varnish. With this technique, you also have complete control over the design. You can choose one from any source; you will simply need to scale it up by tracing

it, then drawing a grid over the tracing and scaling up the squares. It is possible to buy ready-cut stencils with modern or traditional designs, if you wish. It is then easy and inexpensive to test your designs and plans, either by using coloured paper cut to the pattern and stuck to a wall or other surface with masking tape, or by painting the pattern on to a piece of lining paper and pinning that to the surface to gauge the effect. You need apply not one drop of paint until you've got the whole thing absolutely right, which is a great luxury. Stencilling is a process where the

preparation takes longer than the application. However, this is no drawback as half the creative enjoyment of the process lies in the design and preparation of the stencils themselves.

▌ *Cutting stencils* Stencils can be made from a choice of two materials. You can either use clear acetate or oiled stencil-board. Both have their advantages and both require slightly different methods of preparation. If you use acetate for stencils, you will need a special pen to draw on it, a technical pen; for oiled board, a felt-tip pen. A scalpel is necessary in both cases, and a cutting surface – hardboard, plywood, chipboard or, best of all, glass. If you are going to copy a design, you will need tracing paper, and with oiled board you will also need carbon paper and a 5H pencil or fine-gauge knitting needle. In both cases, you need a straight-edge, preferably a metal ruler, and masking tape.

Acetate Using clear acetate for stencils bypasses the need for tracing paper. You can place the acetate directly over the design and then trace the design straight on to the acetate with a technical pen. This is particularly use ful if you are going to work in a variety of colours and need a separate stencil for each colour area. Acetate is most effectively cut on glass, because previous score marks on a cutting board can jolt or turn the blade, and acetate can split if cut suddenly at an awkward angle as a result of snagging the blade like this. Fix the acetate in position on the glass with masking tape to stop it sliding, and protect the edges of the glass with tape to prevent it chipping or cutting you. Hold the knife firmly and cut smoothly and steadily. Cut toward yourself, but *never* place your hand in the path of the advancing knife blade; a scalpel, even moving slowly, will almost always make a deep wound. When cutting curves, turn the board steadily, not your knife hand. Cut small, detailed areas first, but don't try punching them out on glass. Any rough edges can be smoothed with fine abrasive paper. The drawback of acetate is that it has a habit of curling up as you cut it, owing to the heat of your hand, and it can crack and split on tight curves. In general, though, it is rather easier to cut than oiled board.

Oiled stencil-board This has the advantage of being a lot cheaper than acetate, and thicker. It is possible to bevel the edges of the board as you cut it to ensure that paint doesn't seep beneath the rim when you apply the stencil. When cutting the stencil from board, copy the chosen design with a

fine felt-tip pen on to tracing paper, then transfer it on to the board, using the point of a fine-gauge knitting needle or hard 3H or 5H pencil and carbon paper. Leave a margin of at least 1–2½in (2.5–6.2cm) around the design, to ensure that the stencil isn't floppy. As with acetate, fix the board to the cutting surface with tape and cut it in the same manner (preferably on glass). Lining up board stencils is a little trickier than it is with acetate. The best way is to cut them all first and then align them exactly one on top of the other, trimming all the boards to the same size. Also, make small holes in the corners so that you can put a small pencil mark through them on to the wall in order to guide the position of the stencils in the sequence.

Make sure when you cut a motif that you always cut it from one piece of board; don't continue it into another piece as the join will always show when you paint in the pattern. Never cut too near the edge of the stencil boards or they won't be rigid enough to use and may even break up. Also, make sure that if your design goes around a corner, you cut two stencils that allow for this; don't

bend a stencil around the corner – it may work once but the second time you may get seepage of paint, or worse.

■ *Paint and brushes* You can stencil on practically any type of paintwork, provided that it is clean and in good condition. Gloss paint has less key than the other types and so is marginally less suitable, but you can put a matt varnish over it if you don't care about losing the shine. Natural wood needs two thinned coats of matt or satin varnish to seal it, but any other paint surface will take stencilling, provided that it is level.

Similarly, there is a wide choice of stencilling paint. If you are in a hurry there are sign-writers' colours, thinned with matt varnish or mineral spirits; artists' acrylic colours, thinned if necessary with acrylic medium or water; and latex paint, tinted with artists' acrylics or universal stainers. These are all very quick-drying. For woodwork, flat oil-based paint, undercoat or eggshell, tinted with artists' oils and thinned with mineral spirits, are all very suitable but rather slow-drying, though they can be speeded up with a drying agent. In all cases, never make the paint thinner than half and half because if it is watery

LEFT AND BELOW
Preparing a stencil
1 Trace the design on to the stencil-board. If you don't wish to use carbon paper, pencil the design on both sides of the tracing paper and go over it to transfer the graphite on the back of the paper on to the stencil-board.
2 These faint lines can be gone over afresh with a sharp pencil.
3 You can trace a design directly on to clear acetate and cut it immediately. However, acetate cracks easily when you cut it and it is floppy when held vertically against a wall; this allows paint to creep under the edges.
4 When painting, pounce the flat-ended brush vertically up and down, and try not to overload it.

it will run under the stencil and mar the pattern.

Somewhat surprisingly, perhaps, sprays are not very good for stencilling. If you do use sprays, the template must be held down very firmly around the area, for sprayed paint has a marked tendency to seep. If you obey the manufacturer's instructions and deliver the spray horizontally, not at an angle, you lessen the risk of seepage but it can still happen. Sprays are also far more expensive than other mediums, and over an area as small as a stencil it's difficult to get solid, even coverage without sweeping back and forth over the area; this means that you get either seepage or, if you hold the spray close to the surface for denser coverage, drizzling. If you hold the spray well back and don't go heavily into the edges of the motif, then you get a fuzzy, fluffy shape instead of sharp definition. In some circumstances that might be acceptable but not usually; it gives the appearance of a faded decal. Also, you don't save time because you have to go back and forth gradually over the same region, which takes a good deal longer than one good application with a stencilling brush.

Stencilling brushes closely resemble shaving brushes with the bristles chopped off short and square. They are stubby and squat and sometimes known as 'pounce' brushes after their method of application – an up-and-down pouncing or dabbing stroke. They aren't very expensive; cutting down another brush isn't necessary and won't be any cheaper. They come in various sizes, with the smallest ones resembling fitches; some are actually called fitches. Fitches are round in section, flat-ended and used for very detailed stencilling. All of these brushes leave an orange-peel texture on the surface, a slightly grainy appearance. If you really don't want this texture, use a sponge, an ordinary decorating brush, a folded rag or paint pad. An ordinary brush carries the risk of coating slightly under the edge of the motif. Whatever tool you use, the secret is not to overload it. Test on a piece of paper with a test stencil to

ABOVE LEFT *Cut a different stencil for each colour in complicated designs.*

LEFT *To imply age, soften the colour by adding a transparent glaze mixed with a little white pigment to the colour.*

ABOVE *Mellowed colouring improves many simple, naive folk designs. A coat of tinted varnish greys the greens, makes reds* *pink and turns yellows a gentle amber.*

gauge the correct loading.

Other tools You will also need a hardboard or, preferably, glass panel as a palette for the paint, as it is not advisable to put paint straight on the brush from a container; clean rags, appropriate solvent, masking tape, spirit-level, a straight edge, chalk, T-square and plumb-line.

■ *Application* First, you must mark the position of the stencils on the wall. if your design follows a frieze format – that is, a series of patterns following each other along a regular plane, usually at eye level or above – never take your measurements for verticals and horizontals from the walls or ceiling, they are usually out of true. Draw all

horizontal lines in chalk using a spirit-level, and take verticals from this horizontal using a T-square. Then check these with a plumb-line. Next, mark the position of each stencil on the wall with a pencil, using corresponding notches on the stencil to line it up; that is, the pencil mark on the wall should fit into the notch on the stencil.

If you have a freer overall pattern on a floor, or a rug style, then square off the floor with chalk lines and mark the position of each stencil as before. If you have a border around the pattern, it should be equidistant from the wall all round. Lay out the border by drawing parallel chalk tracks; the distance between the lines should be the width of

the stencil templates. Of course, it could be that your room really is very off-square; the best thing to do in that case is to draw a right angle where your border chalk lines meet at the corner, and then when you see just how crooked the room really is, draw the border so that it is somewhere between the two. For example, if the corner of the room is about 41°, and the true corner angle 45°, draw your border at about 43°. Also remember that you can't take motifs round a corner on a flat floor in the same manner as you would on the vertical corner of two walls. You must divide the length of your border by the number of motifs you have and space them out evenly so you don't get one

clogged. When you've finished, clean the stencils and brushes with the same solvent and store the stencils flat. Separate them with tissue paper or baking foil; it's a good idea to keep used stencils because if ever you wish to repeat the pattern it will save you a good deal of time and work. It also means that you can retouch the surfaces at any time, if necessary; stencil work can be retouched with relative ease. Stored properly, stencils last a lifetime.

Remove any pencil and chalk marks from walls with a clean eraser. This is important as you will have to varnish stencillng; any graphite dots will show up under varnish like little hazy flies because the varnish tends to disperse light through its surface and so exaggerate blemishes that would otherwise be unnoticeable. Leave the paint to dry for at least a day – two days for oil-based paints – before varnishing. Two coats of matt or satin-finish varnish are a good idea on walls, and on woodwork and floors they are absolutely essential. Floors look best with satin or matt over gloss varnish to give them a soft sheen, and need at lest three coats, preferably five.

PICKING OUT

Picking out means heightening features that actually exist in three dimensions. On public buildings, this technique takes the form of painting mouldings and other raised surfaces in colours that contrast with or offset the main colouring of the interior or exterior. In domestic interiors, this is rarely advisable Such a treatment can become overpowering and make a lounge look like the central offices of a county court. Used carefully in colouring closely related to the main base colours of a room, however, the picking out of features can greatly enhance a domestic interior. There are two methods for this process, sometimes referred to as positive and negative, the first using paint and the second, tinted glaze.

motif colliding with another on the corner turn. Mark the central point of each motif on the stencil template and the tracks.

When you come to apply the paint, fix the stencil firmly in position with masking tape. Pour out a small amount of paint on to the palette, dip the face of the brush once into it, and then stamp it firmly out on a clean area of the palette or, preferably, another testing surface, to distribute the paint evenly and avoid any heavy or unequal loading. Then, working from the edge of the motif inward to the centre, dab the thinly coated brush straight on to the surface. Rock it back and forth slightly to transfer colour evenly, but don't smear it

across the surface or you'll risk carrying paint under the stencil. When the motif has been filled in, let the paint set for about 30 seconds and then lift the stencil off carefully and *vertically* and transfer it to the next position. If the board is going to overlap adjacent stencils, apply them alternatively to avoid smudging the paint.

If you are working in several colours, always allow one colour to dry before commencing the next. Don't worry about any build-up of paint on the edges of the stencil as this just means you are applying the paint correctly; but clean it off at intervals by wiping it with a sponge or rag steeped in the appropriate solvent, in case it begins to get badly

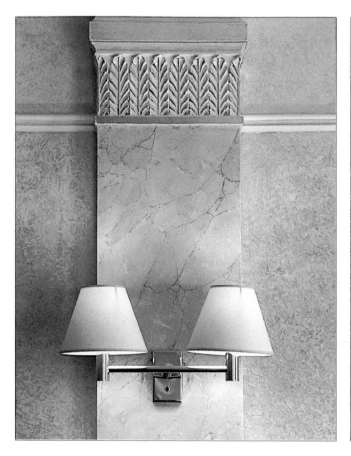

ABOVE *The positive method of picking out. Gilded cornices may appear a little grandiose for most domestic interiors but if handled carefully, with the gilding dulled, they can give a sense of warmth and richness from their reflective surfaces.*

▌ *Application*

Method I When using paint, the first consideration must be the shades used throughout the rest of the room. Remember that mouldings and raised details are an intrinsic element of the whole – they are not the chief objects in the room, nor the whole point of its decoration. It is safest to use a tone of the same colour family as the walls or a major furnishing, or the colour of dominant woodwork. Your choice should be further simplified when you bear in mind that a raised feature painted in a darker colour than its surroundings is going to turn into a silhouette; whereas if it is lighter, the light striking it will cast shadows that outline its features, thus enhancing the appearance of relief.

For painting raised areas, you can use any combination of brushes suited to the size of the details. Decorators use hog-hair fitches but artists' brushes are just as good. You can do one of two things when picking out with paint. The first is to choose a tone slightly darker than the main colour you choose for the raised area. Brush this darker colour into the recesses or background sections of the raised detail and, when that is dry, go over the higher relief with the main, lighter colour, so that the darker shade remains only in the crevices. This approach is easier if the lighter colour is opaque. Alternatively, if the paint is thinner and more translucent, you can paint overall in the lighter colour and then outline the chosen areas with the darker. The first method is rather quicker than the second.

Method II Here, glaze is used to emphasize the same principle of light and shade, but in a considerably subtler manner than with paint. Glaze is also easier to apply. If the whole of the moulding area is finished in an oil-based paint, it can be left to dry and then coated with an oil-based glaze, tinted with oil paint to a darker tone. The glaze can be stippled thoroughly into the recesses. Then, with a rag wrung out in mineral spirits, the glaze can be wiped straight off the raised areas, leaving the darker colour in the crevices to emphasize the shadowy areas, thus throwing the details into high relief.

GLASS PAINTING

Traditionally, the Japanese have been the finest exponents of painting on glass, the lightness and translucency of their brushwork being admirably suited to the technique of placing a thin, coloured liquid on a very thick, rigid and transparent one. In Europe, the Victorians showed a considerable interest in this skill, but only a slender facility for using it. Their approach was an unhappy marriage of minute execution of Dürer-like intensity to the stylized rigidity of stained glass, and the result was rather like two-dimensional taxidermy. This unfortunate result reveals that glass as a painting base offers two distinct options: it can either be used in the manner of medieval stained glass, which makes the most of the light-filtering quality of the medium and makes no attempt to emulate easel painting; or, on the other hand, it can be used for the delicate miniaturism and subdued colouring that has more to do with glass engraving. Painting on glass, as far as interior decoration is concerned, is therefore better orientated to either one or other of these approaches – not both together. However, both methods have a certain amount in common with stencilling, which is relatively straightforward on glass.

To produce a stained-glass pattern, a design can be worked out in the same manner as it is for stencilling, whether or not it is copied from another source. The design should be drawn out on paper or card, the glass simply placed over it and the design traced either in paint or wax pencil straight on to the

RIGHT *Glass painting.* In the nineteenth century, painting glass was frequently used as a substitute for the slower, more costly process of true stained-glass. When glass painting followed the basic forms of stained-glass design, it was often most successful. Much nineteenth-century 'stained glass' is actually painted. When the paintwork became looser in form, the result was often weak and disordered. In this example, the strength and steadiness of the flowing, painted flower-and-stem tracery form a graceful harmony with the genuine stained-glass panels that surround the painted design.

surface of the glass. The best approach is to trace in the outline with an artists' sable brush, using the appropriate colour for each section, and then filling in the area with the right colours.

There are paints expressly designed to be used on glass, with an opaque finish that lets light through evenly, but their consistency varies and one should note the manufacturer's instructions when using them. Artists' oil colour works well too, provided that the glass is cleaned thoroughly first, usually with ordinary window detergent, and allowed to dry thoroughly. Degrees of transparency can be achieved with oil, depending on the amount of solvent added, but all glass with a light source behind it allows illumination of the paint.

The delicate, engraved-glass appearance of finer images can be traced off in the same way, or taken straight off an enlarged (or reduced)

photograph. A result of extraordinary delicacy is possible by laying a monochrome print under glass and working in artists' oil colour in either monochrome greys or sepia over the image, filling areas on the glass to correspond with those on the photograph. The result – when light shines through it – is of a monochrome engraving. It is best to pursue this technique in these colours; to use a large variety of colours can look rather unpleasant as though you'd stuck a large number of coloured decals on the surface, which have started chipping and peeling. But in subdued greys and sepia this never occurs. It is easy to remove unwanted smudges with a cloth or sponge soaked in mineral spirits. If the piece has already dried, paint can be removed with a palette knife; keep the knife as flush to the surface as possible. Glass painting is best protected by placing it under another piece of glass.

GLOSSARY

Alive
A paint or varnish surface that is still soft, wet and in a workable state. When it begins to set and becomes tacky, it ceases to be alive.

Base coat
The paint on top of which other layers are applied, ie undercoat.

Base colour
The foundation or background colour of a design, on occasion also called the ground colour. Off-white, for instance, is the base colour of white Sicilian marble.

Cissing
An effect created by spattering solvent on a paint or varnish surface before it is dry. Mineral spirits are usually spattered on oil-based paint, and water on latex, but the method works well the other way round, too.

Claircolle
Untinted distemper. Size and whiting mixed and applied without colour to give a simple, even, off-white base to coloured distemper.

Crossing off
The final finishing stroke of a *paint* method. The term is interchangeable with 'laying off', except that the latter tends to refer to the whole activity and the direction of the crossing off, whereas crossing off refers to the single action. Crossing off *varnish* means making a stroke at right angles to the rest of the varnish strokes – which are usually vertical – at the bottom of a panel or surface. This stops the varnish running.

Cross-stroke
A criss-crossing stroke in an 'X' formation, usually employed when laying on gloss paint, distressing colour wash, or for other broken colour techniques.

Cutting in
Painting into an angle or on to a narrow surface like a glazing bar. A cutter is a

brush of moderate or narrow width with a flat, chisel shape or hatchet point.

Diffuser
A T-shaped pair of tubes used by artists to diffuse paint or ink in a very fine spray. The base of the 'T' is placed in the liquid; suction is created in the tube by blowing in one arm of the tube, drawing the paint upward, and a second breath disperses the liquid spray from the other arm.

Flatting-oil
A 1:6 mixture of boiled linseed oil and mineral spirits, used to 'float' colour on.

Gesso
A hard, off-white surface traditionally made from hide-glue (usually rabbit skin) and whiting, and often used as a base for gilding work. The best is still made this way, and is applied hot but never boiling in layers, mostly to picture frames and furniture. A cold, ready-to-use liquid form is also available and is reasonably adequate for most decorative work.

Goldsize
A size used in the gilding process. Its clear, viscous quality thickens paint.

Ground
Any surface to which a paint finish is to be applied. The term is also sometimes used to mean the base colour; for example, white Sicilian marble has an off-white ground.

Gypsum-board
A form of plaster board.

Jamb duster
A large, pliable, flat decorators' brush which can be used as a substitute tool for the dragging and combing technique.

Laying off
Another term for crossing off. With paint, it means the uniform direction of finishing strokes as well as the

applications of them; with most types of paint on most surfaces, it should be done toward the light.

Laying on
The action of applying paint or varnish initially, before any finishing strokes. Laying on may be in any direction unless specified, but should never be treated as a brush method for achieving a finished surface, except when you are distressing a colour wash.

Masking tape
A strong, sometimes plastic-coated sticky-backed tape used for blocking off surfaces to protect them from paint. It is also suitable for holding other materials, such as paper and polythene, in place.

Moulding
Raised relief patterns in wood and plaster. In addition, the parallel raised surfaces of doors and architraves, windows and ceiling surrounds are also loosely referred to as mouldings.

Mottle
An irregular pattern similar to that cast by the shadows of leaves. The mottles can be of any size from fist to pin-head. A mottling action is a smudgy stipple created with a brush or sponge by a dabbing action up and down, or with a spray by making irregular patches with random jets.

Over-brushing
Brushing one colour loosely on top of another, either to cover it partly or to alter its tone.

Over-painting
Covering and obliterating one colour with another.

Oxide of chromium
A deep grey-green colour, between moss and mid-olive, similar to terra verde. Originally made from chrome oxides.

▌ Pattern-work
The general structure and flow of a
design, as in stencilling, on mouldings
and lining, or decorative work of any
kind.

▌ Plaster board
A sheet of plaster with a stiff paper
covering on either side. One side of the
board is finished and can be used
without further treatment.

▌ Plumb-line
Traditionally, a cord with a lead weight
at the bottom. The plumb-line is held
steady like a stationary pendulum to test
a true vertical.

▌ Pumice
A light, porous, volcanic rock used for
polishing and scrubbing. Now usually
available in a lump approximately 5in
(13cm) across, it should be cut in half
(with an old saw as it blunts the teeth)
and rubbed on a wet flagstone before
use. It is excellent for washing down
shiny surfaces. Powdered pumice should
be mixed with oil and applied with a
piece of thick felt to achieve a smooth
finish on paint or varnished surfaces.
After using it, the surface should be
rubbed with a lint-free cloth and washed
in turpentine. Pumice gives a soft, deep
gleam.

▌ Retarder
A colourless gel agent mixed with some
water-based paints, like acrylics, to slow
their drying time by inhibiting
evaporation.

▌ Rotten-stone
Decomposed limestone, powdered for
use as a polish. Used with a lint-free rag
and linseed oil, this lubricant should be
rubbed over a surface after a felt-rub
with pumice, sanding or an application
of waterproof abrasive paper. The
surface should then be polished with dry
flour. The result is a soft gleam which
can alter the appearance of a room
considerably.

▌ Spirit level
A wooden or steel rod with a phial in the
centre filled with spirit, used for testing
a true horizontal. When the bubble in
the liquid is in the exact centre of the
phial, the surface is exactly level.

▌ Steel wool
This is available in many grades from
coarse to very fine, and looks like a
bundle of grey hair. Used dry, or with
water or oil, it is highly effective for
rubbing down paintwork, and giving a
key or tooth to smooth surfaces such as
aluminium or galvanised steel. It is
suitable for removing rust, used in
conjunction with mineral spirits. *Don't*
use it on surfaces where you intend to
apply water-based paint, as embedded
particles of it may cause rust under
latex. In this case, use bronze wool.

▌ Stippling
Using a sharp, stiff-bristled brush to
create a pattern that resembles fine grit,
either by exposing a colour used under
glaze, or by applying the colour on top of
another.

▌ Straight-edge
A long ruler. Any stiff, straight object
which offers an undulation-free edge as
a guide.

▌ Tack rag
A sticky cloth designed to pick up
greasy, gritty particles from a surface.

▌ Template
The master or guide drawing for a
design, from which stencils are cut and
tracings made.

▌ Texture (tactile and visual)
Literally, the way a surface feels, usually
to the touch. However, with paint, the
visual texture is often more important.
This means the impression made on the
eye; a surface can evoke roughness
without actually being rough. The term
'surface texture' refers to whether it is
actually rough or smooth to the touch.

▌ Tipping off
Touching the tips of brush bristles on
the side of a paint kettle to eject excess
paint from them.

▌ Translucent colour
Colour which allows you to see the
presence of another beneath, in the
manner that gauze allows you to see
through it.

▌ Transparent colour
Colour which alters the tint of another
beneath it without obscuring it, as tinted
spectacles alter the colour of the sky.

▌ T-square
A T-shaped ruler. The right-angled
cross-bar is placed against the straight
side of a surface, ensuring that a line
drawn will be at right-angles to it.

▌ Under-toning
The tones of background colours. A soft
ochre mottle applied to marble before
the veins and top glazes are applied is
under-toning.

▌ Wash
A thinned coat of colour applied all over
a surface, either over another paint or
as a mist coat when latex is applied to
new plaster.

▌ Water tension
The ripples caused in water-based paint
where patches of it dry at the edges and
don't blend into the adjacent patch
evenly. This is caused by evaporation
from the thin edge of the paint area
being faster than that from its centre.

▌ Wet-and-dry-paper
An abrasive paper designed to smooth a
surface with alternate applications of
lubricated and dry abrasion.

▌ Wet-edge
The alive edge of a paint area. The wet
paint into which the paint of an
adjacent area can be harmoniously
brushed.

I N D E X

ACKNOWLEDGEMENTS

The majority of pictures in this book
were specially commissioned by the
Publishers and shot by John Hesseltine,
Ian Howes and John Wyand.
Additional contributions are from the
following:

Dulux: p 8 bottom

Small Bone of Devizes: pp 10, 138

Elizabeth Whiting and Associates: pp 11,
12, 14, 16, 17, 18, 55, 86, 95, 128, 129,
132, 133, 139

Home Improvement Guide: p 45

Martax, West Point Pepperell: p 103